P9-AGE-686

Taste of Tombstone

A Hearty Helping of History

Sherry A. Monahan

TASTE OF TOMBSTONE: A HEARTY HELPING OF HISTORY
Sherry A. Monahan
© 1998 by Sherry A. Monahan.
All rights reserved. Printed in the United States of America. No part of this publication may be reproduced, stored in a retrieval system or transmitted in any form or by any means, electronic, mechanical, photocopying, recording or otherwise without the written permission of the publisher. Reviewers may quote brief passages to be printed in a magazaine or newspaper.

Publisher: Royal Spectrum Publishing, P.O. Box 228, Ravia, OK 73455, Phone: (405) 371-2904, Fax: (405) 371-9792

Publisher's Cataloging-in-Publication
(provided by Quality Books, Inc.)

Monahan, Sherry A.
Taste of Tombstone : a hearty helping of history / Sherry A. Monahan ; Jennifer Simmons, editor. — 1st ed.
p. cm.
Includes bibliographical references and index.
ISBN: 1-889473-97-9

1. Hospitality industry—Arizona—Tombstone—History. 2. Tombstone (Ariz.)—History. 3. Tombstone (Ariz.)—Social life and customs. 4. Cookery, American—Southwestern style. 5. Cookery—Arizona—Tombstone. I. Title.

TX909.M66 1998   647'.097915
                             QBI97-41217

Editor: Gwen A. Henson, Jennifer Simmons
Book Design & Typesetting: SageBrush Publications, Tempe, Arizona
Cover Design: Running Changes, Phoenix, Arizona
Printing: Affiliated Lithographers, Inc., Phoenix, Arizona

DEDICATION

This book is dedicated to my husband, Larry.

He has always been supportive of every endeavor I have chosen, no matter how unusual. He has listened to my thoughts, hopes and dreams, and encouraged me to follow them. I truly appreciate his support, patience, and indulgence.

TABLE OF CONTENTS

FOREWORD

Ike Clanton opened Tombstone's first restaurant a year before Wyatt Earp arrived in late 1879. However, as Sherry Monahan points out, that restaurant was in the first town of Tombstone on the site of the West Side Mine and should not be confused with the present town of Tombstone, which was laid out six months later, on Goose Flats, March 5, 1879.

From this modest beginning, Ms. Monahan guides us through the establishment of Tombstone's hotels, restaurants, butcher shops, and bakeries for the first ten years. She has even unearthed an order by Ike Clanton for groceries for his restaurant from a Tucson supplier.

Tombstone had only 900 people when Wyatt Earp arrived. Two years later, by the time of the famous street fight outside the O.K. Corral, the population had grown to over 4,000 hungry souls. The restaurants had grown from modest Chinese chop shops to ones serving more sophisticated, continental cuisine. Ms. Monahan details it all with bills of fare and recipes to match.

The history of Tombstone is intertwined with the rise and fall of its eating establishments. The effect of the two great fires in the business district on the hotels and restaurants is covered here in great detail and for the first time.

Anyone who wants history in an appetizing dose will find it here. This book is a delightful guide for anyone who enjoys eating.

Carl Chafin

PREFACE

My "love affair" with Tombstone began the first time I saw it. Blend together that emotion with my passion for writing and cooking, and you have the inspiration for *Taste of Tombstone*.

Being in Tombstone seems to transfer me back in time to the wild days of the 1880s. I am mesmerized and awe-struck, just knowing that I stand on the streets where gamblers and miners once stood. During one of my visits, as I strolled along the boardwalks in the historic town, many thoughts filled my mind. I started thinking about what it must have been like to live in Tombstone back then. What kind of place was it? What did the townspeople do for fun? What did they eat? Where did they eat? Who owned and ran the restaurants and other food businesses in town? Those questions, and more, sent me on a journey back in time—to Tombstone, 1880s style.

While there are many books that revolve around the town's famous residents, little has been written about the hotels, mercantiles and eating establishments during that time. I find it fascinating that the people of Tombstone, during the 1880s, dined in quite a grand style.

When I first thought of Tombstone, I imagined only a desert town with some wooden structures, cowboys, miners, campfires, and chuck wagon grub. First-class dining with silver, china, and linen never entered my mind.

Because of my passions, Tombstone's fascination, and my desire to be connected with that historic town, I have written this book.

Sherry A. Monahan

ACKNOWLEDGMENTS

Even though many individuals have happily helped me along the way, there are three very special people I wish to give the most deserved thanks to. They are Carl Chafin, Steve Elliott, and a "Silver Lady" named Marge, for without them, this book would not be complete.

One of the first phone calls I made when I started gathering information for my book was to **Marge Elliott**, co-owner of Silver Lady Antiques in Tombstone. Marge had never met me, yet she and her husband Steve graciously offered their advice, as well as providing me with invaluable information. Their friendship was an added bonus along the way.

I first met **Christine Rhodes**, Cochise County, Arizona Recorder, when my husband and I were researching Tombstone property records. Christine, and her co-worker Larry, have provided me with valuable resources and helped guide me through all the record books and documents.

Carl Chafin was introduced to me through Christine. Carl's own knowledge, continuous support, and resources were very significant to the completeness of this book. I cannot thank him enough for his generosity, time, guidance, and thought-provoking conversations.

Art Austin, Assistant Park Director of the Tombstone Historical Court House, was instrumental in providing assistance obtaining many historical documents and photographs. (We didn't even mind the little white gloves.)

Various drawings found in this book were provided by my brother-in-law, **Dennis B. Cunningham II**. His skills as an artist are unsurpassed, and his time and hard work are most appreciated.

The true highlight of writing this book came when I located **Bertha Geisenhofer Dalziel**. Bertha is the daughter of one of Tombstone's pioneers, the first man to have a bakery in Tombstone. I will always treasure her enthusiasm, family history, and father's recipes.

Bob Boze Bell, a talented author and artist, has offered encouraging words, guidance, and even support (although he probably doesn't realize it).

Andrea Liebmann-Vinson deserves a special "thank you" for quickly translating Otto Geisenhofer's German recipes.

Victoria Salas, inter-loan librarian of Wake County, North Carolina assisted me in getting several reels of microfilm and books from across the country. She never seemed to mind when I called, which was often, to see if the materials I requested had arrived yet.

During the development of my book, my husband, family, friends and co-workers, especially P.J., listened, tested recipes, and read—probably more than they cared to. I'm sure they tired of hearing me say, "this is the last revision." It means a lot to know they patiently and enthusiastically indulged me.

2 Sheets—Sheet 1.

N. H. DOLSEN.
Kitchen Cabinet.

No. 235,074.

Patented Dec. 7, 1880.

Fig. 1.

Witnesses,
W. H. L. Knight.
W. Blackstock.

Inventor.
N. H. Dolsen.
By Lee Hill
His atty.

X

PROLOGUE

When one thinks of Tombstone, the first thoughts that come to mind are of course, Wyatt Earp, Doc Holliday, the Clantons, the McLaury's, and the street fight at the O.K. Corral (the fight actually happened behind the corral).

While Tombstone is associated with gunslingers, gamblers, and cowboys, it was also a mining boomtown. It had all the modern conveniences, by 1880s standards, including restaurants that were beautifully decorated, and often compared to the finest in San Francisco. Tombstone's restaurants advertised "the most elegantly appointed restaurant in the city," "table supplied with the best the market affords," and "best cooking and polite attentive service..."

Many of the restaurants were decorated with chandeliers, Brussels carpeting, and walnut tables adorned with imported china, cut glass, and stylish cutlery. Dining out, however, was not perfect. Despite the fact that Tombstone patrons ate elaborate meals in a beautiful setting, they still had to suffer through heat, pesky flies, and most annoying, dust from the streets. The unbearable dust did not stop people from dining out though, and they eventually solved the dilemma by sprinkling the streets with water. When water was in great demand, however, none could be spared for the streets.

The meals served by Tombstone's restaurants reflected trends of the 1880s, and did not include today's popular Southwest fare. The *trend* of the 1880s was classic French cooking, but not all of Tombstone's restaurants served French food. The restaurant owners and cooks were from various ethnic backgrounds, and their cooking reflected their heritage. Tombstone's restaurants and chop houses served German, Italian, Chinese, Irish, and "New England" cuisine.

Tombstone's cooks rarely had a problem obtaining fresh meat to prepare their meals because of the wild game, lamb, and cattle available at the local butcher shops. Even though obtaining meat was fairly easy, preparing the meals was not. Credit should be given for the hard work of the people who prepared those meals. Their kitchens did not contain food processors, electric mixers or blenders, and preparing a meal was very time-consuming. Practically everything—mayonnaise, sauces, and stocks—was made from scratch. When you look over the "Bills of Fare" and recipes, consider all the preparation time and effort that went into creating a meal.

In addition to preparing meals for the patrons who dined at their establishments, several restaurants cooked meals for the city's guests staying in Tombstone's jail. The restaurateurs prepared and delivered meals to the jail for the prisoners. It appears that the people of Tombstone ate well, whether it was in the dining room of a restaurant, or behind bars at the jail!

Tombstone offered a wide variety of restaurants and meals. A person dining out in Tombstone probably did not grow tired of it, considering the "Bills of Fare" and the variety of places to dine.

Taste of Tombstone is a brief history of Tombstone and its restaurants, bakeries, meat markets, and grocery stores—all of which contributed to the eating and dining experience. Also included is a collection of recipes you can personally sample in order to experience your own *Taste of Tombstone*. The recipes reflect actual dishes that were on the Bills of Fare and advertised in the newspapers. The recipes and their ingredients are based on what would have been available to Tombstone cooks at that time. I studied several old cookbooks, including some that have been handed down through my family, to ensure they were truly typical 1880s style recipes. Because cooking has changed over the years, a cake or pie recipe from the last century can be quite different from one today. Also keep in mind that, while these recipes are old-fashioned, you don't have to use old-fashioned methods to prepare them. The cooks of the 1880s would understand, and probably even be a little envious.

In addition to researching old cookbooks, I have researched numerous old newspapers, county records, business directories, censuses, and the list goes on. I have not included footnotes, as everything in this book came from these primary resources. Trying to re-create the past in this manner is fun, yet like a jigsaw puzzle. In the end, you hope that you have all the pieces, and they fit together.

The advertisements I've included are copies of those that appeared in the newspapers of the day, and unfortunately, are not perfectly legible due to their age. Nonetheless, I wanted you to get a feel for what it was like to open the newspaper and see the ads as they appeared. I hope that while perusing these pages, you sit and daydream, as I do, about what it was like to dine in Tombstone during the 1880s. Take time now to look back into the dining experience of yesteryear, learn a little, and taste a lot!

Chapter One
1877-1879

There's Silver in Those Hills!

It was the summer of 1877 when Ed Schieffelin first made his silver discovery in the hills of Southern Arizona where he had been told he would only find his tombstone. Ed realized the potential wealth that lay hidden in those hills and eventually recruited his brother Al, and an assayer named Richard Gird to help him uncover it. In February of 1878, the three men set out for the hills where Ed knew he would find his silver fortune. A month later, he discovered the Lucky Cuss Mine, and the rush was on!

Present-day Tombstone, where many of the old mines are, was not the first town established to support the mines. At first, it appeared that water, rather than the mines, would determine the location of the new town. Once a well was sunk at the designated spot where water was found, about three miles away, a sleepy little hamlet named Watervale began to emerge.

By the summer of 1878 two stores in Watervale supported the mining community. The first one was opened by A. W. Stowe and the second by Cadwell & Stanford. In the fall of 1878, many realized that Watervale was no longer a practical location for the town, even though it was the only place near the mines with a well. If a miner needed provisions or wanted a meal, he had to travel from the mines to Watervale. Three miles in the heat and dust was a long way for a weary miner to travel. The next town was settled on the site of the West Side Mine, about 100 yards southeast of the 1880 Fire House. This location was on the hill across from present-day Tombstone. The site prospered and, by the end of the year, boasted a saloon called Danner & Owens, along with a post office. December also saw the opening of the first eating establishment, the Star Restaurant. Its proprietor was none other than Joseph "Ike" Clanton, a participant in the infamous gunfight.

The town site on the West Side Mine was also impractical due to its size limitations, and by March of 1879, some enterprising businessmen realized the need for yet another, and final site for their camp to grow. Another event that may have prompted this move was a windstorm that leveled the west side site.

On March 5, businesses were established on a 320-acre town site, where present-day Tombstone sits. A portion of this site was surveyed, and streets were laid out. The streets that run east and west were named after citizens of territorial or local fame. The ones that run north and south were simply numbered. The new camp evolving in the district was officially named Tombstone. Despite its lack of available water, the town was able to grow rapidly because water was delivered by carts from Watervale— until about a year later.

Most early businesses began in tents, rather than frame or adobe structures. Tents were practical for several reasons. First, building supplies and lumber were limited. Second, mining was a risky and unstable business. Even the first hotel to open in Tombstone began in a tent. The Mohave Hotel, owned by Charles "Charley" Brown would later become Brown's. Charley had quite a diverse career before he came to Tombstone. At the age of nineteen, he left his home in Columbiana County, Ohio and headed for Calaveras County, California. Charley stayed there for ten years where he was engaged in the business of steamboating. He next moved to Virginia City in 1863 and then to Boise City, Idaho, where he was involved in the mining industry and storekeeping. Drawn back to steamboating, Charley went to Oregon, where he remained for several years. When

Charley decided to stay on dry land for a while, he opened the Cosmopolitan Hotel in Portland, Oregon. On the move again, he spent a short time in business at the Battery in San Francisco, then headed for Arizona in 1872. Charley held various jobs and was engaged in different enterprises in Mohave County until 1878, when he moved to Tombstone. He opened his hotel on April 14, 1879, at the corner of 4th and Allen Streets. In the beginning, the Mohave averaged about twenty daily guests, but because of the large number of people continuously flowing into Tombstone, Charley expanded his hotel. He also established the first restaurant in camp. A couple of months later, another eating establishment, the Chinese Restaurant, was opened by Sam Sing.

Mrs. Semantha E. Fallon was another of Tombstone's entrepreneurs who realized the need for additional sleeping facilities. She opened the San Jose Lodging House at the corner of 4th and Fremont Streets. Many miners lived at the San Jose House because Mrs. Fallon offered rooms at reasonable rates. Even with the opening of the San Jose House, Tombstone still couldn't provide enough sleeping accommodations for those arriving in search of their fortunes. Because of the camp's exploding population, yet another hotel was about to open.

The San Jose House and the water wagon
Tombstone Courthouse Historic State Park

In July, Carl Gustav Bilicke, along with his son Albert, opened the Cosmopolitan Hotel in the 400 block of Allen Street. The Cosmopolitan, a tent structure, reportedly offered the very first beds in Tombstone. With the hotel operating at full capacity, "Gus" was able to expand his business shortly after opening. Along with upscale accommodations, Bilicke also offered his guests the pleasant sounds of a recently delivered Steinway piano.

It was apparent that Tombstone was going to be the new town, so Andrew Cadwell and James Stanford made the wise decision to relocate their grocery store from Watervale to the growing new community. They were able to build a brick building on Fremont Street, and they kept a full line of staple goods. Cadwell & Stanford also had competition from P.W. Smith, and James McKean and Isaac Knight who opened their store in September. McKean & Knight kept a full line of groceries and provisions and made a special point of supplying fruits, butter, eggs, cheese, and potatoes from California—needed commodities in a place that was so isolated.

The best and quickest way to ship supplies to Tombstone was by way of the railroad, and then wagon freighters. Since the railroad had not yet reached Tombstone, the goods were delivered to Tucson, which was the closest station, some seventy miles away. From there, wagon freighters or commission merchants delivered the goods. It took the Tucson freighters thirteen hours to make the trip to Tombstone.

Not everything consumed in Tombstone was imported, although it would have been impossible for restaurants and bakeries to operate without delivered goods. Once items such as flour, butter, and eggs reached Tombstone, cooks and bakers created wonderful dishes for their patrons.

Baked delicacies were the specialty of Otto William Geisenhofer, a 22-year-old Bavarian baker. Otto arrived in Tombstone with his older brother Michael and opened the City Bakery, Tombstone's first. By October, the bakery was set up in a tent located at 529 Allen Street, where Otto offered a variety of fresh baked goods including rolls, rye bread, pies, cakes, cookies and candies. He not only sold baked goods to the general public; Otto

Advertisement for Apollinar Bauer's U.S. Market
Tombstone Epitaph, 1880

also supplied the hotels, and mining camps that were set up outside of town. When Otto first visited the United States, he said that "America was going to be the country of the future," and that is why he decided to make it his new home.

In December, German immigrant Joseph Hoefler opened another general merchandise store. Located at 417 Allen Street, the store was built of brick, and like others, was filled with everything to support miners, prospectors, and the increasing number of families arriving.

People living in Tombstone also relied on butchers for their meat supply. Apollinar Bauer, a 35-year-old German immigrant, was one of Tombstone's pioneer butchers. In December, he purchased two lots for $500, where he opened the US Market at 318 Fremont Street. Before opening his shop in Tombstone, Bauer owned a five-acre mill site in Watervale, which he had purchased in February 1879.

The other butcher shop in camp was the Cosmopolitan Market, opened by the Tribolet brothers of Switzerland. Constructed of adobe and located on Fifth Street, the meat market carried all varieties of meats, and specialized in domestic and imported sausages. The five brothers, Abraham, Charles, Godfrey, Robert and Sigfried, though originally involved in the butchering business, didn't limit their interests to the meat industry. They would eventually become general contractors, restaurateurs, landowners, brewers and saloonkeepers. The Cosmopolitan, later called the Eagle Market, was managed by Godfrey, one of the middle brothers, who was later a city council member.

Approximately 900 people lived and worked in the mining camp, that was rapidly becoming the town of Tombstone. It was almost impossible for Tombstone's businesses to expand or build quickly enough to keep up with the huge influx of people arriving daily. It was evident that Tombstone could only grow more prosperous as the new year approached because the existing mines were being diligently worked, and new claims were being staked daily. Even though Tombstone was rapidly growing, and more and more businesses opened, it was still a frontier mining town in 1879. The majority of townspeople were miners, assayers, freighters, and businessmen. Tombstone would eventually become very sophisticated, but it hadn't reached that level yet.

Chapter Two
1880

A Mining Camp Transforms

In 1880, Tombstone's mining camp took on a more civilized look when brick, frame, and adobe building structures took the place of tents. Month by month, businesses such as restaurants, bakeries, ice cream parlors, grocery stores, and meat markets began to line the streets of Tombstone. One of those businesses was the Rural House, opened in January by Henry G. Howe, a Tucson civil engineer and architect. John and Levnie Holly who were from New York ran the dining room of this house. While both Mr. and Mrs. Holly managed the Rural House, it was Mrs. Holly's name that would be associated with it. Mr. Holly had broken a couple of ribs and took laudanum, a common drug of the time, to alleviate the pain. At 6 p.m. on January 23, he was pronounced dead from a laudanum overdose. This loss did not stop Levnie, though, who was left with two young daughters to support. She continued to work in the restaurant business for several years.

In early 1880, Tombstone was being reported as one of the most cosmopolitan silver camps. Even though the camp's businesses were doing well, the town of Tombstone was still in a transitional state. It was believed that once the "boom got a little more underway," the camp would be lively enough for anyone.

California Variety Store   Arizona Historical Society

It was apparently lively enough for William Shilliam, a twenty-five-year-old Englishman, who opened a general merchandise store in town. Located on 4th Street, between Allen and Fremont Streets, Shilliam's opened on February 15. The store carried groceries and provisions, as well as fresh or green* California fruit. William, along with most other merchants, advertised that fresh fish and oysters were a specialty. Rather than competing with the many retail stores in camp, he dealt mostly in the wholesale market. His customers included the hotels, restaurants, dealers, and camps that were set up near the mines.

About the same time, Michael Edwards opened his grocery store, the California Variety Store, at the corner of 4th and Allen Streets.

---

*   Author's note: Shilliam's, as well as others, advertised green fruit. Since dried and canned fruits were often used, green was used to indicate the fruit was fresh—not dried or canned.

The *Arizona Daily Star* frequently printed articles from various Tombstone correspondents, like Wells Spicer, about the progress and activities in Tombstone. Spicer's name might sound familiar because he was the judge who would later preside over the Earp-Cowboy hearing. In February, he reported that the various stages coming to town were well loaded, especially with women and children. He also reported that Tombstone had more restaurants, saloons, gambling houses, and dance houses than any other village, town, or city in Arizona. He wrote, "it is the boss town."

Another business to open in this "boss town," was the City Meat Market. It was a wholesale and retail butcher shop opened by Thomas Patrick Ward, a twenty-eight-year-old Irishman. Thomas' shop was on Allen Street, but his corral and slaughterhouse were located below town, on his ranch along the Barbacomari Creek. The Barbacomari was actually a river, but because it was small, it was referred to as a creek. To support his butchering business, Thomas purchased the ranch on August 26, 1879, from Martin Maloney for $3,000; it included a house, a spring, and a variety of livestock.

By March, Apollinar Bauer, one of the pioneer butchers of Tombstone, had also established his own corral and slaughterhouse. Wholesalers and retailers alike called upon him to make their meat purchases. Bauer was apparently a smart businessman and, when he noticed his competition was increasing, began offering free delivery to all parts of the camp.

Another person faced with competition was Otto Geisenhofer, owner of the City Bakery. Otto's competitor was Joseph Stumpf, who arrived in Tombstone with his wife Flora and their three children, to open the American Bakery on March 15. Joseph, like Otto, was from Bavaria, Germany. The baked goods they both offered were similar and equally delicious. Joseph's bakery was located at 215 5th Street, where he supplied Tombstone's families with breads, pies, and assorted cakes. Even though the two men were competitors, it is doubtful that either of them suffered from lack of business because of the camp's growing population.

1880s Arizona Meat Market   Tombstone Courthouse Historic State Park

By the time April arrived, Tombstone was no longer being referred to as a camp. It was now being called the *town* of Tombstone. In another report to the *Arizona Daily Star*, Wells Spicer reported that new buildings could be seen daily and new foundations for buildings were spreading out all over town. One of these new buildings belonged to Tasker & Hoke, which opened its doors in April as a liquor and general merchandise store. The following month Jacob Hoke left, and on May 4, George Pridham purchased a half interest in the business. The store became known as Tasker & Pridham's, although some of the town's people still referred to it as Tasker & Hoke's. Located at the corner of 5th and Allen Streets, Tasker & Pridham's quickly became one of the leading general merchandise stores in Tombstone. The store carried a variety of goods, including groceries, produce, California wine, as well as foreign wines and liquors.

Tasker & Pridham's also attracted the mining clientele by keeping a full line of items to outfit a miner.

Tombstone eventually had many items, such as fruits and vegetables available locally, but that wasn't the case at first. The people living in town shopped at general merchandise stores, such as the Boss Store, P.W. Smith's, Nellie Cashman & Jennie Swift's Tombstone Cash Store, and Tasker & Pridham's, to buy their imported goods. Imported goods meant anything that was not locally available. The grocery stores of the 1880s hardly resembled the grocery stores we know today. A Tombstone grocery store more closely resembled a mercantile store, where a merchant not only carried food, but provisions for miners and prospectors as well. By June, Tombstone had approximately sixteen mercantile stores. Since a majority of their customers were associated with the mining business, a large portion of the grocery or mercantile stores allowed their patrons to purchase on credit. Purchasing on credit was almost a necessity when wages were paid so sporadically. Some of the merchants kept a running bill at their store for credit paying customers, while others required the customer to maintain a credit book. The patrons brought their books with them to make their purchases on credit. Since this was risky for the merchants, they charged higher rates to buy on credit. Those who could pay cash were offered items at a discounted rate.

Large quantities of goods were constantly being delivered to Tombstone. In April, the *Arizona Daily Star* reported that P.W. Smith, one of Tombstone's merchants, had received a train car full of merchandise. This merchandise included clothing, dry goods, liquors, hardware, and groceries. Smith and other merchants bought a large portion of their goods from California companies; however, they also purchased items from mercantile firms in Tucson. L. Zeckendorf had one of the largest firms in Tucson. In fact, he did so much business with Tombstone merchants, that he eventually opened a branch office. It was reported that Tombstonians would soon be able to get their merchandise a little quicker. Plans had been made for the railroad to extend its service closer to Tombstone in June. The new

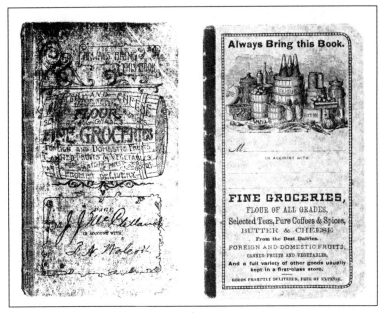

1880s Tombstone merchant credit book

Tombstone Courthouse Historic State Park

railroad town, about twenty-eight miles away, was named Benson. Merchandise that once had been delivered to Tucson could now be shipped to Benson, and from there, the commission merchants and stages would transport it to Tombstone. This trip took nearly five and one-half hours, less than half the time it took from Tucson.

As the town grew, and people continued to arrive in Tombstone with the hope of striking it rich, the concern over water availability was growing. The water being brought to town was largely consumed by the building trade, thereby creating shortages for bathing and other common uses. Tombstone eventually had its own water source, but not for a couple more dry and dusty months.

Although the dust made things uncomfortable, it didn't prevent hopeful entrepreneurs from opening businesses. More restaurants had opened in town by the time the desert flowers began to bloom. There was Lukini & Staglono's chop house, Peter Marcovich's Queen Chop House, William Smith's restau-

Carleton's Coffee, Oyster and Chop House,
523 Allen Street.
MEALS AT ALL HOURS AT ANY PRICE.
Every thing First-class. The most comfortable Eating House in the City. San Francisco and Tombstone Daily Papers. Give us a call and we will guarantee perfect satisfaction. LUNCHES PUT UP FOR TRAVELERS.

Advertisement for Carleton's   *Tombstone Epitaph*, 1881

rant, Wong Fong's restaurant, and the Arcade Restaurant, which was opened by Joseph Pascholy, a thirty-year-old Swiss immigrant. Shortly thereafter, Frank Herbert Carleton, twenty-eight, opened Carleton's Coffee, Oyster, and Chop House at 523 Allen Street. Like many others, Frank served everyone, including miners, gamblers, and businessmen. Some of the items he offered were coffee, ice cream, oysters, and chops, as the name of his restaurant indicated. Patrons could also have paid a visit to the Gem Coffee and Ice Cream parlor on Allen Street if they desired hot chocolate or ice cream. Another restaurant to open by mid 1880 was the Boston House. Mrs. Merrill was the proprietor of this business located on 4th Street. Not long after opening the Boston House, she left to become the proprietor of the Cosmopolitan Hotel Dining Room. The Cosmopolitan Hotel's dining room was said to be one of the finest in the Territory.

CAKE OR PIE WITH FRENCH COFFEE FOR 15 CENTS AT THE BOSTON HOUSE.

Tombstone Epitaph, 1880

By June, the mines were producing more quality silver ore than anyone had anticipated. As a result, more miners, businessmen, and their respective families were settling in Tombstone. The town had more and more people to feed and entertain. Some of the entertainment included theater shows, grand balls, private parties, and dining out. By this time, there were fifteen restaurants and dining halls in town to support a population of approximately 2,000 people. Some of the newest restaurants in Tombstone were Delmonico's, the Golden Eagle, an Italian restaurant, the Bodie restaurant, and the Star Restaurant, which was being run by Lucy Young and Belle Sullivan.

Tombstone witnessed the birth of many new businesses. Existing enterprises were changing and experiencing growing pains. Charley Brown, the owner of Brown's Hotel, was one of those going through changes. He hired Tucson city architect and restaurateur H.G. Howe to design an upper story for his hotel. By June, he had torn down his wooden-frame hotel, and construction of the new building had begun. The new two-story structure was built of brick, and could accommodate 100 to 150 guests. Now that Mr. Brown's hotel was quickly growing, he was in need of a manager. As luck would have it, while browsing through the want ads, he found George Bayley's request for a position as a manager in a hotel or restaurant. Charley subsequently hired George to manage both Brown's Hotel and its restaurant, which became known as Bayley's Restaurant. Mr. Bayley was a good choice because he brought twenty years of experience from the California hotel business. The restaurant

Brown's Hotel & Bayley's Restaurant   Arizona Historical Society

and kitchen were next door to the hotel, at 403 Allen Street, and could feed 300 people at any given meal. Charley was not only a wise businessman, but also a devoted husband. Shortly after construction of his new hotel, Mr. Brown gave the business property to his wife, Caroline. The transaction was completed on July 8, and the consideration for the deal was not money, but rather with "his love and affection." Just two months later, Charley and Caroline borrowed $2,000 from Safford, Hudson & Co. Bank; this may have been to pay for the newly completed additions.

The Cosmopolitan Hotel was also making improvements during this time. The Bilickes had a second story addition built that offered superior accommodations. The most notable improvement was the construction of a front verandah that was handsomely decorated with orange trees. Around the time of his improvements, Gus planned an invitation only party. The festivities were held in the dining room of the hotel, and the guests danced to music played by Lee's band. The Cosmopolitan had also had a ball just two months before that hadn't ended so pleasantly. In front of the Cosmopolitan, Mike Killeen was murdered by either Frank Leslie or George Perine, depending upon which story one believes. It seems that Mike was a little angry with Frank who was dating Mike's wife. When the couple appeared together at the ball, as the account of the murder goes, words flew, and the bullets shortly followed, leaving Mike dead. Neither Frank nor George was convicted of murder, but there were strong indications that George Perine actually killed Mike Killeen. Frank and Mike's widow were eventually married.

Nearby, the Rural House was undergoing changes. Mrs. Holly, the owner, resigned to operate the dining room of the soon-to-be-opened Grand Hotel. She must have planned her move for months, because in January she had requested that a deed for the Grand be recorded in her name. George Rutledge and James Crowley purchased the Rural House from her in June. Shortly thereafter, on July 12, Rutledge and Crowley dissolved their partnership. Mr. Crowley remained the proprietor of the house, and he hired Mrs. Carrie Hanson, a thirty-two-year-old

Mrs. Holly requests deed recordation

Arizona Historical Society

native of Denmark, to take charge of the dining room management. Carrie was no newcomer to this field; she was quite experienced. When she first came to Tombstone, she worked for Semantha Fallon at the San Jose House, and then she became the proprietor of the Miner's Boarding House that was located at the corner of 5th and Toughnut Streets. Mrs. Hanson was apparently a no-nonsense businesswoman who preferred to have any outstanding debts with her house satisfied promptly. At the end of the August, she placed a newspaper ad requesting that those who had not satisfied their debts with the Rural House do so immediately. While Mrs. Hanson was taking care of her portion of the business, Mr. Crowley, however, was not. He apparently ran into a cash flow problem with M. Calisher & Co., one of his suppliers. M. Calisher & Co. filed attachments and garnishments against Mr. Crowley in mid 1880. However, by early September, the litigation filed against him was released. Carrie Hanson left Tombstone a couple of years later to open her own restaurant in Johnson, Arizona.

With hope and determination, residents continued to improve Tombstone. Their desire to succeed was evidenced by the town's growth. Until this point, the town's greatest drawback, had been the shortage of water. However, by the end of July, water pipes had been laid by the Sycamore Springs Water Company, which began producing small quantities of water. With water more readily available, Tombstone's assessed property value increased. Two months later, the water company advertised that it was prepared to deliver water for domestic consumption at the uniform rate of one-and-one-quarter cents per gallon. The company claimed that the water was free from organic impurities, suitable for laundry, and was better than the hard water previously used in Tombstone. The people of Tombstone could choose to obtain their water from the street main, or they could have it delivered by wagons. Sycamore Springs Water Company also made it quite clear that they did not intend to readily accept Mexican money for payment of water rates. If exceptions were made, and Mexican money was accepted, it's face value would be discounted by ten percent.

At this time, the Western Union Telegraph lines reached Tombstone. Western Union's arrival was a significant event, for it meant that Tombstone and the outside world would have access to each other.

By the time Tombstone was receiving water, Apollinar Bauer, of the US Market, had taken on a business partner. His partner was none other than Henry Clay Hooker, the territory's cattle baron and owner of the well-known Sierra Bonita Ranch. It was at this ranch that Wyatt and Warren Earp, and others rested in 1881 while in pursuit of the men who had robbed the Kinnear stagecoach.

Bauer and Hooker appropriately called their new business venture Hooker & Bauer's, and their shop was located at Bauer's original business location of 4th and Fremont Streets. In August, Bauer sold half of his lots numbered four and five to Hooker for $300. Even though this deed was drawn up in August, it wasn't recorded until July 5, 1881. Nonetheless, they promised to supply the best beef from American fed cattle and vowed to "defy competition," an easy task, since Henry Clay Hooker's cattle were considered the best.

Meat markets and butchers were very much needed in Tombstone, as they were in any 1880s town. Most of the butchers purchased their cattle by the hundred and had their own corrals and slaughterhouses. By the time summer arrived, there were four butchers in town. A little over a year later, that number had doubled. Many of them advertised that their cattle were "American." This supposedly meant that the cattle was not rustled illegally across the Mexican border, as many were at the time— but not all butchers were honest advertisers. Some cattle were considered so "hot" you barely needed to cook it! Local business owners and residents made frequent, almost daily, trips to the meat market simply because they couldn't stock up as there was no place to store the meat. Tombstone had ice, and iceboxes for storage, but the technology hardly compared to the refrigerators and freezers of today.

Ice was an important commodity in Tombstone. It was a necessity for families as well as businesses, such as saloons, restaurants, and ice cream parlors, which relied on ice for a variety of obvious reasons. In a June report to the *Arizona Daily Star*, Wells Spicer reported that Tombstone was receiving four large chunks of ice daily. One of the businesses that delivered ice to town was the Tombstone Stage Line, run by Ed Swift. His company was an agent for Paul Moroney's Ice Company, which sold ice to the residents of Tombstone. However, the following month ice would be more readily available to those living in Tombstone. The *Arizona Daily Star* printed an article from the July 4th issue of Tombstone's *Nugget* regarding plans for an ice factory near Tombstone. The article stated that over the past few months several individuals, namely the Gird brothers and F.A.J. Diss, had announced their idea of establishing an ice factory in the district. The site they chose was near Charleston, considered to be the most centrally located town for ice shipments. They were so confident that their ice factory would be built that they already had five, ton capacity ice machines shipped to them. They also stated that they intended to sell the ice at reasonable rates, so everyone could afford it.

The *town* of Tombstone was fast becoming known as the *city* of Tombstone. On September 9, its third and reportedly its finest hotel and restaurant opened. The new hotel, called the Grand, was centrally located on Allen Street. An *Epitaph* reporter was given a pre-opening inspection of this new hotel and restaurant. The title of the article, "Tombstone's New Hotel—The Most Elegant Hostelry in Arizona," sums up his observations.

The article stated "...the first thing to strike the eye is the wide and handsome staircase, covered by an elegant carpet and supporting a heavy black walnut baluster." The reporter also wrote that, "A heavy Brussels carpet of the most elegant style and finish graces the floor; the walls are adorned with rare and costly paintings; the furniture is of walnut, cushioned with the most expensive silk; and nothing lacks, save the piano, which will be in place shortly."

The reporter continued with the dining room description, "Three elegant chandeliers are pendant from the handsome center pieces; walnut tables, extension and plain, covered with cut glass, china, silver castors and the latest style of cutlery are among many attractions of this branch of the cuisine. Thence into the kitchen, where we find the same evidences before mentioned; an elegant Montagin range some twenty feet in length, with patent broiler, hot and cold water—in fact all the appliances necessary to feed five hundred persons at a few hours notice are present. This department is presided over by Messrs.

Grand Hotel, 1880   *Arizona Quarterly Illustrated*

Devern and Whitehead, which is a sufficient guarantee of its efficiency." The lessee of the Grand, Mrs. Levnie C. Holly, was formerly the manager of the Rural House, where she had gained a reputation as a skilled caterer. On September 15, George Parsons, a miner, entered in his journal that he breakfasted at the Grand Hotel. He noted "the best place I've been thus far in the territory. Something like a hotel. Best meal yet and best served. Popular prices too—only four bits."

The Grand wasn't the only business to open in Tombstone that month; it just happened to gain the most attention. Mrs. M.L. Woods leased a building that once housed a furniture store, and then placed an ad for a waiter. On September 17, she opened the Melrose Restaurant at 426 Fremont Street. The *Epitaph* published an article on Mrs. Woods that stated she was a camp pioneer and her restaurant was one of the largest and most elegantly appointed. Unfortunately, the Grand's opening overshadowed her restaurant opening.

In October, Nellie Cashman, a native of Ireland and previous owner of Delmonico's in Tucson, leased the Arcade Restaurant.

Ms. Cashman was also the owner of the Nevada Boot and Shoe Company in town. Shortly after Nellie leased the Arcade, she had a new landlord. Joseph Pascholy, the former owner, sold the lot, all the buildings, fixtures, utensils, and Nellie's lease, to Thomas Dewers of West Chester, Pennsylvania. Mr. Dewers paid $6,000 for this purchase, not a bad profit for Mr. Pascholy, who had only paid $1,100 for it just six months earlier.

Pascholy owned a lot on Fremont Street, between 4th and 5th Streets, an adobe house on Toughnut and San Pedro, the Bell Mine in the Huachuca Mountains, a one-third interest in the Salano Mine in Tombstone, and the Occidental Saloon on Allen Street. The front of the saloon contained a restaurant, run by Aristotle Petro, known as the Occidental Chop House or Occidental Restaurant—depending upon which newspaper you were reading. It seems that the *Epitaph* preferred chop house, while the *Nugget* always used restaurant. Regardless of what it was called, the chop house, located at 429 Allen Street, served extravagant French cuisine.

Even more surprising than the French food being on the menu was the fresh fish and shellfish that most of the restaurants frequently offered. The seafood was packed in ice and brought in by train from California and the East Coast. Many merchants advertised that oysters shipped by express from Baltimore were available for purchase.

Tombstone's early pioneers were beginning to experience success. Otto Geisenhofer purchased the lot where his bakery and brewery were located for $520 from Charles Rodig, and in October he replaced his tent with a brick building. Otto's business seemed to be doing well, and just two months prior, he purchased a two-room house on the corner of 2nd and Bruce Streets for $280. This was quite an accomplishment since most of Tombstone's residents lived at their business locations, in hotels, or at boarding houses, because homes were few and far between.

By this time, the Sycamore Springs Water Company, in an effort to bring uniformity to the distribution of water, posted its water ticket prices in the local paper. In order to buy water from the company, you needed to purchase tickets. The ticket prices were:

3 gallon tickets—27 for $1.00 or 13 for 50 cents
4 gallon tickets—20 for $1.00 or 10 for 50 cents
5 gallon tickets—16 for $1.00 or 8 for 50 cents

Tickets could be purchased from the drivers of the company's wagons, at the company's office, or at the agent's office. They were redeemable at the selling rates and Tombstonians redeemed their tickets where the water was delivered within the town limits.

Tombstone's atmosphere was not only enriched by the convenience of available water, but also by the social fund-raising functions held by the churches. On October 7, the Presbyterian Church held a "Grand Concert" at Gird's building on the corner of 4th and Fremont Streets. The musical entertainment provided was the production of an original song entitled "Tombstone Camp" with words by the town's founder, Ed Schieffelin.

Tombstone's population was so transient, that change was familiar to the city—not only in people, but in businesses as well. Some businesses, like the Rural House closed, but were quickly replaced by others. In October, Mr. Edward Rafferty opened the Miner's Restaurant at the Rural House's former location, 521 Allen Street. His restaurant not only served food, but also doubled as a retail and wholesale liquor business.

The Cosmopolitan, one of the town's first hotels, was well on its way to being established as one of Tombstone's best. The Cosmopolitan had a fine dining room attached that had been presided over by Mrs. Merrill. However, in early November, J.W. Cameron announced he had taken over the dining room and renamed it The Cosmopolitan Restaurant. Cameron placed a "Bill of Fare" in the *Epitaph* for his Thanksgiving dinner on November 24 that included all the traditional favorites. The Cosmopolitan Restaurant would later become known as the *Maison Doree*.

The Methodist Church was another place where one could dine on traditional Thanksgiving fare. The tables, set at six o'clock, were loaded with turkey, urns of cranberry sauce, mince and pumpkin pies, frosted cakes, jellies, jams, fruits, and steam-

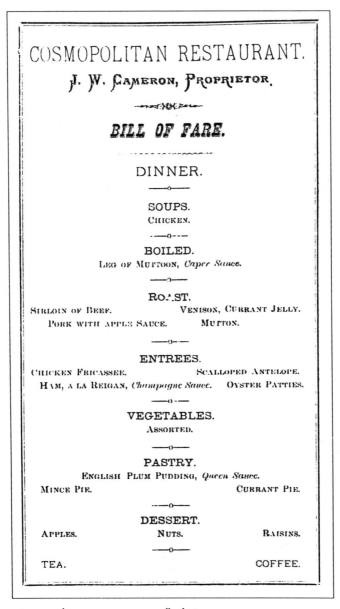

COSMOPOLITAN RESTAURANT.

J. W. CAMERON, PROPRIETOR.

BILL OF FARE.

DINNER.

SOUPS.
CHICKEN.

BOILED.
LEG OF MUTTON, *Caper Sauce.*

ROAST.
SIRLOIN OF BEEF.   VENISON, CURRANT JELLY.
PORK WITH APPLE SAUCE.   MUTTON.

ENTREES.
CHICKEN FRICASSEE.   SCALLOPED ANTELOPE.
HAM, A LA REIGAN, *Champagne Sauce.*   OYSTER PATTIES.

VEGETABLES.
ASSORTED.

PASTRY.
ENGLISH PLUM PUDDING, *Queen Sauce.*
MINCE PIE.   CURRANT PIE.

DESSERT.
APPLES.   NUTS.   RAISINS.

TEA.   COFFEE.

Cosmopolitan Restaurant Bill of Fare   Silver Lady Antiques

ing kettles of coffee and tea. The tea, probably purchased from one of the town's merchants, was said to be for the spinsters in town.

The Methodist Church also held fund-raising events, such as bake sales, however, not all the cakes were sold at the church social. The leftover ones were auctioned the next day to the highest bidder. George W. Atkins was a thirty-five-year-old miner who lived in Tombstone, and was smitten with a young lady in town. George had his eye on one particular cake for his sweetheart, and said he intended to buy it for her, even if it cost him $25! The cake George wanted was frosted and decorated with a one-legged cupid.

Tombstone's Mayor, John Clum, was also present at the bidding, and knowing that George wanted this cake, saw an opportunity to increase the church's profits. The auctioneer lifted the cake and asked, "How much am I bid for this cake?" The Mayor responded with a bid of $5, to which the auctioneer said, "What! Only $5 for this elegant cake, with tulle fringe around the edge and frost *a la Pompadour* on its head?" In response to this comment, George bid $7, and then the Mayor bid $9. The auctioneer was still not satisfied with a $9 bid, and said, "This cake has a cupid on it; true it only has one eye, and the other looks like a ten-cent adobe, but love is said to be blind. I'll admit it only has one leg, but Cupid flies and doesn't walk." George was still set on purchasing this amorously decorated cake for his sweetheart, so in a whispering tone, he bid $10. The auctioneer asked for a bid of $12, which the Mayor gladly offered. The auctioneer ended the bidding by saying, "The Mayor takes the cake." George sadly left the auction without his Cupid cake, and the Mayor left, failing to see the humor in the auctioneer's final comment.

The merchandise that arrived in Tombstone came from everywhere imaginable: California, the East Coast, Asia and Europe. The variety of merchandise was endless, too. Ham from the Westphalian region of Germany, molasses from Louisiana, and tea from Japan were just some of the many goods imported to Tombstone.

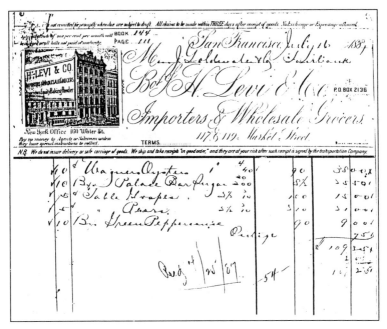

Invoice for goods shipped from California

Tombstone Courthouse Historic State Park

One of the newest grocery stores opened in late 1880, was H.E. Hills & Company, located at 217 4th Street. Their advertised list of groceries was quite impressive and included extracted honey, Japanese Tea, deep sea codfish, and New Orleans molasses.

By the end of 1880, Tombstone had established itself as a community that was well on its way to success. This was the year that Tombstone could proudly say that it was no longer a rough, frontier mining camp without sophistication. The city could now attract people with its churches, schools, a theatre, fine hotels, and first-class restaurants. Tombstone was on the edge of prosperity, with no end in sight to its potential. Those who were willing to take a chance could reap the benefits and live the good life!

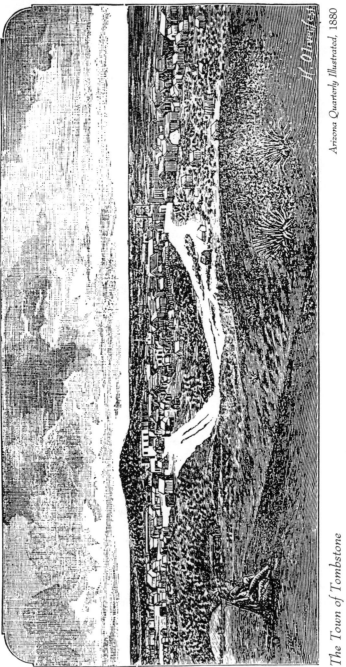

The Town of Tombstone

Arizona Quarterly Illustrated, 1880

CHAPTER THREE
1881

A VERY
EVENTFUL
YEAR

The year of 1881 would prove to be one of new starts and re-building for Tombstone and the people who lived there. To begin with, the butchering firm of Hooker & Bauer did not endure, probably because Edward Hooker, Henry's son, opened a butcher shop on Allen Street by the beginning of the year. It was also at this time that Apollinar Bauer and his wife, Maria, borrowed $800, which was secured against the business, from Safford, Hudson & Company. This loan may have been to buy out Henry Clay Hooker's interest in Hooker & Bauer's. The following month, Apollinar sold his 160-acre ranch near the Dragoon Mountains, thirteen miles from Tombstone, to his brother Bernard. He sold his butchering business to Jacob Everhardy on March 7, 1881. Apollinar went into a new line of work for a while. He used his own driving team to haul adobe and sand for the local masons. After his brother, Bernard, opened a butcher shop on September 27, Apollinar worked for him. Bernard and James Kehoe partnered together to open the Union Poultry and Meat Market at Apollinar's old shop location. Their business must have been a success because they were able to purchase 600 head of American cattle from Mr. E.B. Frink in the Sulphur Springs Valley. It was also reported that Bauer and Kehoe had one of the "neatest" delivery wagons in Tombstone.

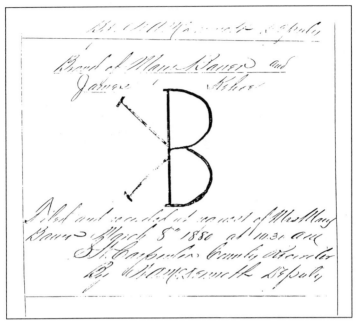

Bauer and Kehoe cattle brand

Arizona Department Library Archives

The Territory of Arizona, in an effort to help reduce cattle rustling and to protect ranchers, enacted a law on February 12 that regulated the business of butchering. The law stated that those in the business of butchering or slaughtering horned cattle, were required to follow certain regulations. These laws included keeping a record book that described each animal, its brand, age, weight, and the person from whom the animal was purchased. It also required a butcher to file a $1,000 bond with the County and to keep the animal's hide available for inspection for ten days from the slaughter date. The purpose of keeping the hide was so the brand on the animal could be identified. If the butcher failed to comply with these regulations, he would be charged with a misdemeanor, and if convicted, was subject to a fine from $10 to $100 for each offense. Butchers were not the only ones in the cattle business who were affected by the new laws. Some of the other regulations dealt with cattle theft, the driving of stolen cattle, rustling, and the sale of stolen cattle. All of these offenses were considered grand larceny and punishable by spending one to ten years in the Territorial Prison in Yuma, Arizona. However, a rustler in those days would probably have preferred spending time in jail, rather than having a disgruntled rancher punish him, which probably would have involved a rope necktie!

It was also in February that Cochise County was formed, and Tombstone became the county seat. These changes greatly impacted the city's growth and its future in many ways. While Tombstone was preparing to handle the many facets of being a county seat, residents and business owners alike were scrambling to ensure that their deeds and other legal documents had been properly recorded in Pima County. If their deeds weren't properly recorded, they may have had a problem when they tried to transfer real estate later on.

As more people became residents of the newly formed Cochise County, more businesses opened to support them. One of those businesses was opened in February by John C. Fitzhenry, who established his grocery and provision store at 216 5th Street.

Letter requesting books needed for new recorder's office

Arizona Historical Society

Fitzhenry's regularly advertised that fresh vegetables, turkeys from Kansas City, celery from Los Angeles, and oysters from Baltimore were available for purchase. The people of Tombstone could either stroll by the stores or review the local papers to see what the merchants were advertising. They would have seen ads for fresh oysters, salmon, and a variety of fruits and vegetables. Fitzhenry's later became known as Fitzhenry & Mansfield's, when Russel Mansfield, son of the lieutenant governor of California, joined the business. Fitzhenry and Mansfield not only worked together, but they also purchased side-by-side residential lots on Bruce Street in March for $37.50.

Along with being a busy merchant, John was a member of the Ancient Order of United Workmen (A.O.U.W.) and held the position of Deputy Grand Master. Many of Tombstone's businessmen belonged to a variety of social clubs.

Fitzhenry and Mansfield weren't the only businessmen investing in Tombstone real estate. Mr. Hills, of H.E. Hills, leased two lots on 1st Street from the Vizina Mining Company for $300, on March 2. Joseph Stumpf, of the American Bakery, bought the corner lot next to his bakery on 4th and Fremont Streets in March. His purchase proved to be profitable, just one month later. The Campbell's, Robert, a twenty-eight-year-old Irish immigrant, along with his wife Bridget, opened the New Orleans Restaurant and liquor saloon at 219 4th Street, next to the American Bakery. They quickly decided to expand and purchased a thirty-by-twenty-foot portion of Joseph's lot that adjoined theirs, for $300.

Jacob Everhardy, after purchasing Apollinar Bauer's business, opened his shop and called it the Fremont Street Market. By July, he was in full operation at 404 Fremont Street. His patrons could choose from a variety of meats, including beef, mutton, pork, sausage, and game. In addition to his large selection of meats, Jacob also offered free delivery to all parts of the city.

Thomas Ward was another butcher in town, and one of its earliest. He decided that a move was necessary, and on March 17, sold his ranch to another butcher named G.W. Lang for the sum of $300. Lang eventually partnered with Jacob Everhardy. Although Ward sold his ranch, he remained in the butchering business in Tombstone.

When local residents craved sweets, they paid a visit to Earl & Banning's shop, which opened around the middle of the year. The shop, located on 4th Street, near Fremont Street, advertised that ice cold soda water, fresh homemade candy, and ice cream were always on hand. A few months later Samuel Shaw joined Banning to form the Ice Cream Saloon at the same location. The ice cream shop not only sold ice cream to the public, but also supplied ice cream to the churches, which would in turn sell it for fund-raising events. Just as Earl and Banning were opening their ice cream store, one of their most important commodities was being reduced in price. Antonio Gallardo, a twenty-four-year old former carpenter, established a ranch on the San Pedro River with plans to supply Tombstone with "the best quality milk" at only sixty cents a gallon or twenty cents per quart. Shortly after Earl and Banning started their business, the Crystal Palace Ice Cream Saloon opened on the corner of 4th and Allen Streets. The owner advertised that ice cream, French lunches, choice of wines, and light summer refreshments were available. The Crystal Palace also offered elegantly furnished private rooms where ladies could dine. The ice cream saloon was not connected with the liquor saloon of the same name. The Crystal Palace Saloon didn't assume that name until the summer of 1882—after the disastrous fire of May 25 destroyed the ice cream saloon.

Tombstone had a number of women who ran successful businesses in town. One of them was Mrs. Florence Hemsath, who operated the Bon Ton Restaurant, located at 321 Fremont Street. Other female proprietors were Mrs. Jessie Brown, in charge of the Grand Hotel, Mrs. M.R. Christie, who ran a lodging house, Mrs. Frances Cunningham, of Delmonico Lodgings, Miss Kate Killilea, who ran the Golden Eagle Restaurant, and Mrs. Lucy Young, who owned the Palace Lodging House. Aside from running businesses, many of Tombstone's women were involved in the town's religious well being. The number of

Kate Killilea's business license   Arizona Historical Society

churches now totaled four: Catholic, Methodist, Presbyterian, and Episcopalian.

June proved to be a fateful month for many in Tombstone, especially for Kate Killilea who owned the Golden Eagle Restaurant. First, on June 6, someone broke into her restaurant, chloroformed her, and relieved her of $500 she kept under her mattress. To add insult to injury, just sixteen days later, on June 22, she lost her restaurant to a fire. Kate's dreams went up in smoke that day, and she was forced to leave. It's likely she left because she suffered a $1,000 loss and had no insurance to re-build. The fire swept through half of the town's newly developed business district and destroyed four blocks of businesses that were located east of 5th Street. The fire also engulfed the Arcade Restaurant, but the luck of the Irish must have been smiling on Nellie Cashman; she had leased the Arcade to Julius Albert Koska earlier in the month. Unfortunately for Mr. Koska, the fire completely destroyed his new restaurant, and he suffered a $2,000 loss.

Another one of the fire's victims was Tasker & Pridham's merchandise store, which suffered a $2,500 loss in the blaze. Fortunately for them, and many others, they were able to rebuild in a relatively short period of time. They also signed a ninety-nine year, $500 lease with the Mountain Maid Mining Company to occupy their existing location at the corner of 5th and Allen Streets. Otto Geisenhofer's City Bakery, valued at $1,000, was destroyed less than a year after the construction of its new building. The bakery didn't stand a chance of survival, since the fire started only a couple of stores away in the Arcade Saloon. Many other surrounding businesses were lost to the fire as well. The Brooklyn Restaurant was destroyed, McKean & Knight's merchandise store suffered a $25,000 loss, Fitzhenry's lost all of its stock, valued at $2,000, the Tombstone Restaurant and Saloon suffered a $1,000 loss, the National Chop House was burned out for a loss of $1,000, Carleton's Restaurant suffered a $1,000 loss, the Eclipse Bakery was destroyed, Frank Yaple's ice cream and candy store suffered a $500 loss, the Nevada Restaurant lost $1,000, and Cadwell & Stanford's grocery store's losses amounted to $7,500. The total of all reported losses to the town was approximately $250,000.

The Campbell's New Orleans Restaurant may have been spared from the fire's flames, but it didn't escape damage. The restaurant's kitchen was crushed when his neighbor's adobe wall fell into it. The Campbells were able to settle with their neighbor, who paid them $500 for the damage. Mrs. Campbell, who was in the kitchen at the time, was not injured, and was reported "fortunate to be around to tend to her usual duties."

Almost as quickly as the fire destroyed Tombstone, it was rebuilt, despite the fact that most businesses were not insured. The smoldering remains of the business district were cleared away, and construction of new buildings was begun shortly after the ground had cooled. In fact, only a month after the fire, half of the destroyed business district had been rebuilt. Some of businesses were able to rebuild at their old locations, while others relocated elsewhere in the city. In spite of Tombstone's tremendous losses, it went on to have some of the best businesses and eating establishments a city could offer. Otto Geisenhofer was able to rebuild his City Bakery, and he continued to provide Tombstone with baked goods. The *Epitaph* acknowledged his re-opening by stating that "His breads, pies, and cakes will be just as palatable as before he was burned out." The mercantile store of Cadwell & Stanford was also rebuilt. Another merchant who had no insurance and lost everything to the fire was John Fitzhenry. John was, however, able to quickly re-open his store on June 27 at 6th and Fremont Streets.

Many of the town's restaurants destroyed by the fire were able to emerge from the destruction. On June 29, Peter Marcovich re-opened the Queen Chop House. He signed a monthly lease with Andrew Cadwell and James Stanford to occupy the former site of the Star Restaurant on Allen Street for $100 per month.

The fire did not prevent people from immigrating to Tombstone, and they continued to arrive daily. None of the existing, over-populated hotels were lost to the fire, in fact, just before the blaze Tombstone welcomed another, much needed one. The new hotel was called the Russ House, and it was located directly opposite some of Tombstone's earliest mines on the corner of 5th and Toughnut Streets. It was first opened by Sol T. Anderson and Jacob Smith to serve as a boarding house, with a first-class saloon attached. The Russ House would later prove to be one of Tombstone's most popular hotels and restaurants, but under different management.

The management at the Can Can Chop House remained stable for quite some time under the watchful eyes of Andrew Walsh and William Shanahan, who had opened their restaurant by July. Andrew David Walsh was an Irish machinist and William W. Shanahan, before partnering with Walsh, was the proprietor of the Comstock Saloon on 5th Street. Their chop house was situated at 435 Allen Street in 1881, but the following year relocated to the Occidental Restaurant's old location at 429 Allen Street. While the history of the Can Can Chop House revolves around the partnership of Walsh and Shanahan, it has also been said that Ah Lum and Quong Kee were the owners. These men were not the owners of *this* Can Can Chop House on Allen Street, but they could have been the owners, when the Can Can Cafe was later located at the corner of 4th & Allen Streets during the 1890s and early 1900s.

Tombstone's other restaurant's histories are easier to follow. Mrs. M.L. Woods owned the Melrose Restaurant, but only kept it for a little less than a year, and then sold it to James Noble on August 8. Mrs. Woods took a break from Tombstone, and went to visit her relatives in Jersey City. Mr. Noble, the Melrose's new owner, had previously been the proprietor of the US Restaurant located at 312 Allen Street. In September the *Epitaph* ran an advertisement showing the Bon Ton Restaurant for sale. This is probably when John Grattan purchased it from Mrs. Hemsath. Unfortunately the restaurant didn't fare too well, and John went on to try a variety of occupations over the next couple of years. He was a bartender, a clerk at the Key West Cigar Store on Allen Street, and even tried his hand at mining.

Not all of Tombstone's businesses were a success. Both Fritz Stenk and Hannah Brooks closed their bakeries almost as quickly as they opened them. They were both issued a three-month business license, but when the tax collector tried to pay them a visit shortly thereafter, he ran into a problem. He found that Hannah Brooks was out of business, and Fritz Stenk was nowhere to be found. Some people only made it as far as getting a business license and never actually opened. This situation was not uncommon in a town where businesses were as likely to fail as to succeed.

Some of the larger, successful restaurants in Tombstone, like the Russ House, the Occidental, the Grand, and the *Maison Doree*, repeatedly placed a "Bill of Fare," in Sunday's newspapers. A "Bill of Fare" resembled a restaurant's menu and outlined the meals served that day. Most of the other restaurants either ran small ads or did not advertise at all. Whether they simply felt they did not need to, or could not afford to, is uncertain. When viewing the advertisements, especially the "Bills of Fare," one suspects that they were read to the reporter who printed them, since many of the words are spelled as they might sound. The "Bills of Fare" also listed the cost of the meal, which ranged from twenty-five to fifty cents. Whether that was reasonable or expensive depended on what one did for a living. The proprietors of the restaurants realized that many patrons worked odd hours, therefore, many of them provided meals at all hours of the day and night. Others restaurants kept to the traditional, scheduled dinner hours, much as we do today. The other reason that not all restaurants were open day and night was due to the cost of business licenses. Business licenses were more expensive for those who opted to keep their restaurants continuously open—so not everyone did.

As local patrons reviewed the newspaper to see what the specialties were, they may have needed a French dictionary, because several of the restaurants served French food, which was quite trendy for the time. Some of the "Bills of Fare" were printed in French, which would have made it difficult for most residents. Mrs. Brown, of the Grand Hotel, finally realized this and, the *Epitaph* reported, "They have taken a new and very sensible departure by publishing its bill of fare in English, instead of French." The other restaurants quickly followed suit. The Grand changed more than its newspaper ads; the hotel also changed its appearance. In July, Mrs. Brown contracted for an addition to be put on the hotel. When it was completed in August, she had a new upper story, as well as five patented fire escapes. Mrs. Brown traveled to San Francisco to purchase the necessary furniture for the new addition. She also saw that her patrons eating needs were taken care of, when she leased the Grand Hotel Dining Room to Henry Holthower, who was the former cook at the Can Can. With these latest improvements, stylish furnishings, its own dining room, and a cordial hostess, it's not surprising that the Grand was patronized by so many. Even the notorious cowboys were impressed with the Grand's accommodations and frequently stayed there. The guest register often included the names of Ike Clanton, Phineas Clanton, Billy Clanton and Johnny Ringo. Despite all of these interior improvements, Mrs. Brown was arrested for violation of the nuisance ordinance because she allowed "filth" to accumulate behind her hotel. The Chief of Police testified that she had been given several notices, which she had ignored. Mrs. Brown pled ignorance of the notices and illness, as an excuse for non-compliance. The complaint was discharged in exchange for a promise to immediately clean up the mess.

Maison Doree, which in French means "house of gold" or "golden house," was originally the Cosmopolitan Hotel Dining Room connected with the hotel of the same name on Allen Street. The restaurant regularly advertised that fresh oysters were always available, and that it only employed French cooks. It was not uncommon to publicize such things; it was actually considered smart advertising at the time. Some of the restaurants also advertised "no Chinese employed" and "white cooks only." George C. Marks owned the *Maison Doree*, and Isaac "Little Jakey" Jacobs was in charge of the kitchen. Jacobs was a twenty-seven-year-old Russian whose catering skills were well known. One of his duties was to procure meat for the restaurant. Either Jakey didn't like to hunt, or he didn't have the time, so he placed an advertisement in the local paper soliciting wild game. Jakey's appeal to the public worked, and shortly thereafter, he was preparing delicious meals for his patrons.

Meanwhile, Aristotle Petro, owner of the Occidental Chop House, hired Alvan S. Young as its new cook. Alvan was an experienced Mississippi River steamboat cook, which, according to the *Epitaph*, was sufficient guarantee of his culinary skills. The arrangement must not have worked out, however, because a couple of months later, Mr. Petro hired his former French chef, Louis Rich, who had left the Occidental earlier to spend the summer in Hermosillo. Perhaps Alvan was the cook who had been involved in a fight at the restaurant a few months earlier, prompting Aristotle to hire a new cook. Mr. Petro enhanced his restaurant by re-papering and renovating the restaurant and by adding a private ladies dining room in the front. He was quite clever when he placed his advertisements in the local newspapers. He captioned one of his ads "A thing of beauty (is) a joy forever," a quote from poet John Keats, while another stated that "Al racked his brains for new dishes until his hair begins to fall like the Autumn leaves." [sic] The Occidental's Bills of Fare were remarkable and specialized in classic French cuisine. This cuisine must have taken hours to prepare, and explains why Aristotle would have required the services of a chef. The Occidental, as well as many others, also specialized in fresh seafood like oysters and even lobster.

GROCERIES!

FOR EVERYBODY.

Notwithstanding there has been an advance in prices of many goods in our line, we are still selling

GROCERIES

—AT—

Bottom Prices !

And we invite you to call and get our figures before purchasing elsewhere.

Do Not Forget !

That we are Sole Agents for the sale of

LOS GATOS FLOUR !

Acknowledged the very best Flour in the Territory.

SPECIAL.

50 cs. Tomatoes, gal. cans, 75c. each—regular price 90c.

Good Japan Tea, 50c. per lb. regular price 75c.

Better Japan Tea, 70c. per lb. —regular price $1.

Best Japan Tea, 90c. per lb.— regular price $1.25.

H. E. HILLS & CO.,

Cash Grocers,

317 FOURTH STREET.

Tombstone Epitaph, 1881

Tombstone had been attracting big businesses from the East and California. By September, H.E. Hills was an established grocery, when the successful Los Angeles produce merchants Woodhead and Gay opened a store in Tombstone. Since these wholesale producers maintained stores in several locations, including Phoenix and Tucson, they hired Frank N. Wolcott to manage their Tombstone store. Woodhead & Gay's often advertised items such as California figs, oranges, nuts, apples, and fresh fish were available.

There was always a supply of fruits and vegetables available in Tombstone, but the same could not be said for eggs. The *Daily Nugget* reported, "Fresh eggs are very scarce in town. An oyster is said to lay 125,000,000 eggs in one season, and if a man could get a cross between the two, he would have a fortune."

Tombstone's businesses were generating a fortune, but it wasn't from eggs, it was from the mining business. The town was bustling with surveyors, barbers, tailors, newspapermen, doctors, attorneys, saloonkeepers, and restaurateurs. It now had three water companies and gas lighting to illuminate approximately twenty-four restau-

Meal ticket for Mack's, 1881

Silver Lady Antiques

rants; this total did not include the lunch stands in the saloons. Two restaurants opened on Fremont Street in October: Mrs. Gleason's Fremont Street Restaurant, and Mack's Chop House, owned by James McGrath, who had just returned to Tombstone from a restful vacation.

The Russ House, on Toughnut Street, could have been considered new as well, since Joseph Pascholy partnered with Nellie Cashman by this time to take over its management and ownership. The *Tombstone Epitaph* ran a feature article on the Russ House shortly after it opened stating that, "The homelike features of the Russ House will be appreciated in a land where homes are scarce, and where bachelors are unpleasantly numerous." The first dinner at the Russ House was on October 3, and more than 400 people dined at the grand opening. Even though the business was prospering, just one month after opening, Nellie announced that she would be selling her interest in the Russ House for personal reasons. It would not, however, be the end of Nellie's association with the Russ House.

Shortly after opening its doors, the Russ House obtained a competitive new neighbor. On Toughnut Street, just west of the Russ House, a new boarding house opened, and was run by Mrs. L. Sewell and Mrs. M. P. Anderson. Since it was simply a boarding house, it is doubtful that the Russ House's owners were worried, or that their business suffered.

Another new restaurant celebrated its grand opening, on October 22, when John Bogovich, an Austrian cook, and his partner, M. Bruce, opened the Rockaway Oyster House at 207

5th Street. The businessmen's first advertisement tantalized the palette of the reader with items such as fresh fish, chicken, and, of course, oysters, the restaurant's namesake. The Rockaway offered its patrons their choice of raw, stewed, or fried oysters.

Tombstone's restaurants were part of everyday life in the city, but they and their owners also played a role in Tombstone's most dramatic event. In October, a series of events finally led to a violent end in the streets of Tombstone. October 26, the Earps and Doc Holliday faced the Clantons and the McLaurys during the infamous street fight in the vacant lot behind the O.K. Corral. Even though the fight was between the Earps, Doc Holliday, the Clantons and the McLaurys, it affected the entire town. Wyatt Earp and John "Doc" Holliday were eventually arrested, and a lengthy preliminary hearing ensued. After they were arrested, the judge set their bail at $20,000 each. Many of the businessmen in town were friends with the Earps and Holliday and showed their support by rallying together and collectively raising the needed money. Some of those businessmen were Charley Brown, owner of Brown's Hotel, who put up $2,000, and Albert Bilicke, owner of the Cosmopolitan Hotel, who put up $1,000. The hearing was another story altogether, and many people testified that they saw what happened. For example, Mrs. M.J. King was a dressmaker who had been in Bauer's meat market at the time of the shooting. There she was, paying a friendly visit to her local butcher shop, when suddenly several gunshots were heard! Mrs. King testified that she had witnessed Doc Holliday and the Earps passing by while she was in Bauer's shop. It was also outside this meat market that a conversation between Johnny Behan, the Cochise County sheriff, and Wyatt Earp took place, directly after the shooting had ended.

Bauer's name was associated with a more melodious sound—the music of the German zither. Apollinar was quite proficient at playing the instrument, and gave lessons to some of the other townspeople, who referred to him as "Zither Bauer."

While some of the town's residents were enjoying the sweet sounds of the German zither, others took pleasure in sipping coffee and eating pastries at Tombstone's newest bakery and restaurant. Earlier in the year, Julius Caesar, a thirty-eight-

Bill to City of Tombstone from NY Restaurant for prisoner's meals—
signed by Virgil W. Earp

Arizona Historical Society

year-old native of Hanover, Germany, opened the NY Bakery, Restaurant and Coffee House. Julius advertised that first-class meals and fresh baked goods could always be procured at the NY Bakery, located at 415 Allen Street. He also prepared pastries for Tombstone's parties and social functions, of which there were many. In addition to the regular business from his shop, Mr. Caesar supplemented his income by preparing meals for Tombstone's prisoners. At the end of the each month, Mr. Caesar submitted a bill to the City Marshal or City Council for reimbursement.

Around the corner, Shaw & Company opened coffee parlors on October 20 at 220 4th Street. The new business replaced Banning & Shaw's Ice Cream Saloon; the two men had dissolved their partnership on October 3, 1881. Mrs. A.C. Davis had also opened an ice cream saloon on Fremont Street. Her saloon was described as an "elegant little bijou" where many ladies and their escorts chose to eat ice cream.

It's a good thing there were so many "sweet" places in Tombstone, because Isaac "Little Jakey" Jacobs made frequent trips to them all. The story is that Jakey had a sweetheart whom he showered liberally with gifts of bonbons, candies, fruit, and cake. Apparently these goodies weren't enough to keep Jakey's girl true to him. One day he called on her, and much to his

55

surprise, found her sharing his latest installment of treats, with his hated rival! Understandably, he was upset, and was quoted in the *Nugget* as saying, "It's not fair. A fellow can make love to another man's girl, but it ain't right to eat all the goods things he gives her." The *Nugget* concurred with Jakey's statement.

Because Jakey was a caterer in town and Thanksgiving would soon arrive, he had to put his personal woes behind him to prepare for the celebration. While he was busy at the restaurant, others were preparing to cook traditional turkey dinners at home that probably required a trip to a local butcher shop or grocery store. Fitzhenry, the grocer, had placed a notice in the newspaper advertising he had just received a "fine lot of dressed turkeys from Kansas and a large invoice of Booth's Baltimore oysters." His advertisement also advised that, "All judicious and economical housekeepers will find it to their advantage to call as early as possible, as these luxuries are in great demand, being the finest ever brought to this place." While some people rushed to Fitzhenry's to get their turkeys and oysters, others, like the Campbells, traveled out of town, while still others dined out. The newspapers were filled with businesses advertising Thanksgiving items and dinner. Probably the most notable Thanksgiving dinner event occurred at the *Maison Doree* where the Tombstone Engine Company gave a "Ball Supper." The proprietor, George Marks, made the occasion especially festive by having menus printed on satin. An *Epitaph* reporter must have attended the festivities because on the following day the paper reported that a "daisy dinner" was served by Little Jakey, despite his recent heartbreak.

Holiday celebrations, as well as everyday life, were more enjoyable because Mayor John Clum had discovered a solution earlier in the year for taming the dry and dusty streets of Tombstone. When the mayor saw the miners dumping buckets full of water that they had removed from the mines, he proposed to salvage it to dampen the dusty streets. The streets, specifically Allen and Fremont, between 2nd and 8th, were then regularly sprinkled with water making travel decidedly more pleasant. People could cross the streets without soiling their clothes and the gusty winds no longer kicked up blinding clouds of dust.

ELITE RESTAURANT.

Mush and Milk	10	Mississippi Corn Bread	5
Oat Meal and Milk	10	Corn Batter Cakes	5
Cracked Wheat	10	Buckwheat Cakes	5
Hot Rolls	5	Milk Toast	10
Dry Toast	5	Tea or Coffee	5

COOKED TO ORDER.

Porterhouse Steak	25
Sirloin Steak	20
Rib Steak	20
Beefsteak	15
Mutton Chop	15
Sausage	15
Fried Bacon	15
Brains, in batter	15
Beefsteak, Spanish	15
Lamb Cutlet Breaded	15
Fried Ham	15
Pork Chop	15

COOKED TO ORDER.

Veal Cutlet Breaded	15
Liver and Bacon	15

EGGS.

Ham and Eggs	20
Ham and three Eggs	25
Two Fried Eggs	15
Three Fried Eggs	20
Omelette, two Eggs	15
Omelette three Eggs	20
Scrambled, two Eggs	15
Scrambled, three Eggs	20

DINNER BILL OF FARE.

SOUP.

FISH.

ENTREES.

ROASTS

Beef	Mutton	Veal	Pork

VEGETABLES.

PIE AND PUDDING.

COMMERCIAL PRINT, 211 FIFTH ST.

Arizona Historical Society

The following month, George Marks sold the *Maison Doree* to Constantine Protosaltis, a twenty-year-old native of Greece, and Mr. Riche. Its caterer, Isaac "Little Jakey" Jacobs left and opened the Grand Restaurant, which, incidentally, was not associated with the Grand Hotel. He rented the room next door to Brown's Hotel entrance on 4th Street from Charley Brown.

Just as Jakey was preparing to open his new restaurant, there was talk of a beef shortage. Ranchers said that unless large shipments were imported, beef cattle would be in short supply within the next three months. Some of the largest ranchers were moving their stock to other areas because of a recent Indian scare, and the depredations of cattle thieves.

The threat of a beef shortage didn't stop the owners of the Elite Restaurant at 215 Allen Street from enlarging their restaurant's accommodations for their guests. The *Epitaph* reported that the new dining room was one of the largest and best appointed in Arizona. The owners of the Elite may have been quick to see the need for increased accommodations, but their foresight wasn't as keen when it came to paying their taxes. According to the 1881 Assessment Roll of the City of Tombstone, one of the Elite's owners, D.J. Bucksley, was being sued by the City of Tombstone for not paying taxes at the end of the year.

By the end of 1881, the water that surfaced in the mines was no longer a problem; it was even seen as a good thing. Meanwhile, the railroad was closer to Tombstone, reaching towns along the San Pedro River area. From these towns, merchants were able to have their goods delivered; Fairbank, was only nine miles away, and Contention, was ten miles from town. Wholesale distributors transported the freight by wagon from the two towns to Tombstone.

Tombstone was a town filled with things to amuse its residents. On one December evening alone, there were meetings of the firemen, the Odd fellows, the City Council, the literary, and the debating societies. Christmas was also a time for celebration, and the *Epitaph* announced that a grand Christmas tree celebration would be held at the Methodist church. Others events were a ball theater, dancing school, and two private parties. Events like these were evidence that Tombstone continued to be a lively place.

CHAPTER FOUR
1882

THE CITY
GROWS
SOPHISTICATED

Some of the local butchers started the new year by forming the Butcher's Protective Association of Tombstone on January 28. The members of the committee resolved that it was their intention not to trust any hotel, restaurant, or person who bought on credit for more than one week. All outstanding bills would have to be settled by the following Monday. The original members of this association were: Jacob Everhardy (President), Thomas P. Ward (Vice President), G.W. Lang and Ernest Storm, Robert Clifford and Mr. Collins, Joseph Meyer, James Carruthers and Mr. Parker.

One of the butchers who was not associated with this group was Apollinar Bauer. He relocated his slaughterhouse in February to a large arroyo north of the city along the Sycamore pipeline, which was very convenient for his business. In June 1881, he transferred his four lots on Fremont Street to his wife Maria for $1. Apollinar went back into butchering, doing business as A. Bauer, wholesale and retail meat dealer. Shortly after he relocated his slaughterhouse, Apollinar purchased a new and very stylish delivery wagon that helped him transport meat packages to town. Apollinar had previously worked for his brother, Bernard, and James Kehoe, who were scheduled to appear in court. The proceeding November they had filed a complaint against Mrs. M. V. Gleeson, owner of the Fremont Street Restaurant. Between September 4 and October 6, 1881, Bauer and Kehoe delivered meat she ordered, but she had failed to pay them the $77.23 she owed. The judge ordered Mrs. Gleeson to appear in court on January 31 to plead her case or pay her debt in full.

It was also at the start of 1882 that an unusual crime took place at Brown's Hotel. It seems that someone, for reasons unknown, tore the last two pages from Charles Brown's day book and stole his hotel ledger. Mr. Brown was so outraged that he placed an ad in the *Epitaph* offering a $75 reward for the arrest and conviction of the perpetrator.

At the same time that Brown's Hotel was relieved of some of its belongings, the Grand Hotel's new owners were filling theirs with many new ones. Shortly after arriving in town, Mr. and Mrs. Archie McBride leased the hotel from Comstock & Brown for $650 per month. The newlywed McBrides were from Prescott, Arizona, and had lived in Tucson for a short time before coming to Tombstone. Comstock & Brown originally leased the hotel to W.D. Crow, J.E. Palmer, and John Chenowith in November of 1881. The lease, however, had a stipulation that required the lessees to either purchase the existing furniture in the Grand from Comstock & Brown or to purchase new furniture by the first of January. The three men must have failed to comply with this stipulation, and on January 13, the McBride's leased the hotel. The McBrides spared no expense to make it a "grand" hotel. Archie went to a furniture manufacturer in St. Louis, Missouri, to make his purchases. The freight bill alone amounted to about $3,000. Mrs. McBride was also involved in the Grand's new look, and while her husband was busying himself with the furniture delivery, she acquired a large quantity of window plants. The plants were placed near the windows of each hall in the upper floor of the hotel. The porch on the second floor was also ornamented with ivies and other choice climbers that eliminated the empty spaces between the windows. In preparation for its opening, the Grand's owners fitted up the unoccupied store in the west front of the hotel as the dining room. The Grand's former owner, Mrs. Jessie Brown, left the hotel in February. While she was packing to move, the hotel was turned upside down—boxes were scattered everywhere. She moved to Socorro, New Mexico, where she opened that town's newest hotel.

Mr. McBride had apparently worked himself so hard that he was taken ill in February with a bad cold and went to Yuma, Arizona, to recover. Mrs. McBride remained at the hotel to prepare for its opening, and Mr. Julian Piercy of Prescott, Arizona, arrived to help her. As in previous years, an *Epitaph* reporter was given a tour of the newly renovated hotel. He stated, "one cannot help but smile on entering the handsome parlor, the scene which greets the eye is so pleasing. This apartment has been furnished in red, according to the latest style, and is really beautiful. In fact, the neatness in all the furniture, the bright pretty designs of the carpets make all the rooms appear so cozy that you want to move right in." Despite the fact that Archie went to Yuma for his health, he was not able to recover from his illness, and passed away on May 15, 1882, leaving his new wife to run the hotel alone.

The Grand Hotel may have been the talk of the town, but Jakey's restaurant was also something to marvel at. Jakey's restaurant was described as elegant, with six private dining rooms, a public dining hall with four tables, and a family dining hall with the same. The window of the restaurant even sported a fountain in which the basin was filled with rocks, plants and fish! Little Jakey's former boss, George Marks, had left Tombstone after selling the *Maison Doree*, and was now in charge of his father's mercantile business in Contention City. In addition, the *Epitaph* reported that Marks had "struck it rich" at a mine in Sonora, Mexico. Jakey wasn't so lucky. On March 27, 1882, it was announced that the Grand Restaurant had financially collapsed.

Even though Jakey and George Marks were no longer associated with the *Maison Doree*, it continued to be a popular place in Tombstone. The restaurant's new chef was Louis Rich. The Ancient Order of United Workmen (A.O.U.W.) was impressed with Louis' reputation and hired him to cater their banquet. Rich previously worked at the Occidental where he was known for his artistic culinary skills; he showed them off by molding butter into forms of animals for the occasion.

Dining out was a popular pastime in Tombstone, but the ladies of the Methodist Church held a fund-raising event that offered an alternative to the usual restaurant fare. In the beginning of the year, the ladies prepared an old-fashioned "New England" lunch that offered the rich flavor of home cooking. The food was served at the Miner's Exchange, in the room adjoining the courthouse, between eleven and two o'clock.

The ladies home-cooked lunch may have been popular, but it certainly didn't put any of the town's restaurants out of business. The Occidental continued to serve its usual fare, which included steak. The *Epitaph* printed a funny story on that subject. A boarder at the Occidental gazed upon his plate one morning and then said, "Is there a reliable physician stopping in this house?" "Yes, Sir," said the waiter. "Good surgeon, too, eh?" "Believe so, Sir." "Then you just see if he is in his room before I start on breakfast. I had a brother choked to death on a steak like that once, and I'm bound to take all the necessary precautions."

Although Tombstone and its businesses were still growing and prosperous, not everyone in town was successful. Frank Carleton was one of the unfortunate ones. First, he lost his restaurant to the fire of June 1881. Second, in July, he attempted to kill Frank Diss. The crime Frank committed, wasn't one of money, but one of passion. Apparently Mrs. Carleton had been having illicit relations with Mr. Diss, superintendent of the Tombstone Ice Works. Even though she had left her husband, and was living with Mr. Diss, she was still married to Frank. Frank must have a had a problem with this situation, and paid a visit to the Ice Works one Sunday evening, where he found his wife, an unidentified woman, and Mr. Diss sitting in the office. He appeared at the door, fired his pistol and missed. Frank's second shot was more accurate and landed squarely in Mr. Diss' abdomen. While Frank was promptly being arrested, Dr. Matthews attended to Mr. Diss' wound, which was thought to be fatal. Mr. Diss eventually recovered from the shooting. These misfortunes may have prompted Frank to leave Tombstone in March. Although he left Tombstone, he stayed in the restaurant business and purchased the Montreal House in Johnson, Arizona, for $400, from E.H. Mayero. Frank apparently wasn't too successful there, or maybe he just missed the excitement of Tombstone. At any rate, he returned the following year and worked as a steward in Tombstone's hospital.

In March, Robert and Bridget Campbell returned from San Francisco, and they established a new eatery called the St. Louis Restaurant. When they left in 1881 their New Orleans Restaurant became the property of Mr. and Mrs. D.H. Jones. A couple of months later, the Campbell's were able to move the St. Louis Restaurant to their old restaurant location.

At the same time, John L. McCullough opened his restaurant, called the NY Coffee Saloon and Restaurant. Located at 203 4th Street, he offered breads and pies, and served coffee with cake for fifteen cents. It was reported that the food he prepared was well cooked and neatly served.

The Grand Hotel's new restaurant was soon to be opened by Misters Fraser and DeGraw. It was a spacious, first-class dining hall serving dishes that were described as the very daintiest and fancy. The restaurant occupied the new front addition that had originally been designed for a store. The high ceiling provided a bright and airy feeling. The display window had borders of plants surrounding the centerpiece of wild game, fish, and choice cuts of meat to tempt the hungry.

After dining out at the Grand, some of the residents attended a performance of biographical sketches at the local school. The students performed "The Life of Garfield" and "Biography of Lafayette." The students also sang "Chick Chickery."

While Tombstone had its social gatherings and fancy restaurants, it was not crime free. As with any growing town, Tombstone had its share of criminal activity, aside from killings. One day in March, a man was arrested for being drunk and disorderly, and another was arrested for creating a disturbance in town.

There was certainly a great deal of activity in Tombstone's businesses, but it was especially evident in the city's restaurants. Most of the people involved in the food industry didn't stay in any one place for very long, which caused turnover in existing businesses and generated the opening of new ones. The American Restaurant on Allen Street, which was operated by Mrs. Dill, was one of the newest additions, along with Mrs. M.L. Woods' boarding house. Mrs. Woods, who had previously owned the Melrose Restaurant, was charging $8 per week for room and board and serving fifty-cent meals in her house at 617 Fremont Street. Edmund Saul had run the Melrose, since October 1881. Another French restaurant was opened by Ed Terroll & Company at 510 Allen Street, next door to Cadwell & Stanford's grocery store.

Grocery stores were also experiencing an increase in business, as well as competition. The firm of P.W. Smith had recently received a shipment of 40,000 pounds of freight from California and the East. His competition was from the new firm of Chandler & Forsyth's, which opened on February 6 at 328 Fremont Street. As the new merchants were receiving goods for their store, they decided to post some of the prices in the newspaper. Because they were new, Chandler & Forsyth's placed several different ads in the various Tombstone newspapers. Their March 25 ad in the *Commercial Advertiser* was very large and advertised cheese, bananas, oatmeal, eggs, butter, tapioca, macaroni, crackers, potatoes, and onions for sale. The two announced the name of their store would be the C.O.D. House. Their motto was "Cash Talks" or "Cheap for Cash." The editor of the paper remarked that, "By paying cash you will save ten percent, which is quite an item." J.G. Brown also quietly opened a family grocery store, where H. E. Hill's grocery store had been at 217 4th Street. Woodhead & Gay's, prospering, relocated its business to a larger store on 5th Street, near Fremont. McKean and Knight, who were two of the first men to open a grocery store in Tombstone, had assigned their business to August Baron.

Another mercantile firm in town, M. Calisher & Company, was long established by that time, but the business wasn't doing

CITY ITEMS

Chandler & Forsyth's Prices.

The following are some of the prices at the cash store, 328 Freemont street. Prices on other articles will appear soon :

6 lbs. cube sugar $1
7½ lbs. brown $1.
Butter 80 cents a roll .
Fresh eggs 3 doz. $1.
13 bars soap $1.
8 lbs. Sandwich Island rice $1.
Jellies and jams 35 cents.
Table fruits 37½ cents.
Fresh roasted coffee 25 cents.
Sweet oranges 30 cents a doz.
Choice lemons 25 cents a doz.
Choice limes 50 cents 100.

Chandler & Forsyth's Advertisement   *Tombstone Epitaph*

well. In February, David Calisher was forced to assign stock back to the company's creditors and by early March, the creditors had almost completely sold the assignment through private sales. Calisher, in a desperate attempt to salvage something, did the unthinkable. On the night of March 5, he attempted to set fire to his building in the hope of collecting the insurance money. The store was insured for $1,800 and the adjoining shoe store for $800. To accomplish his deed, he left kerosene-soaked papers in an oil can sitting under some wooden shelves. Fortunately for the town, policemen Kinney and Joseph Poynton noticed the flames and sounded the fire alarm. The hook and ladder team arrived on the scene and tore the burning shelves down. They weren't able to extinguish the flames with water because the hydrants had been temporarily turned off. Calisher must have known about this, because the shut off notice had been published in the paper the day before. Although Calisher failed at his attempt, the fire of the preceding June still remained fresh in the minds of the townspeople. When they realized what he had done, they cried, "Lynch him!" "Hang him!" The feeling was so strong that Calisher sought police protection. The police promptly arrested him and offered him refuge in the county jail. Had Calisher succeeded, Tombstone could have suffered another disastrous fire. His bail was set at $1,500. The following month, Bisbee merchant, E .T. Hardy, announced he had taken over Calisher's old store. The *Epitaph* reported, "Another live businessman, one who has confidence in the town and acts on his convictions."

Tombstone's businesses continued to do well thanks to the mining industry. Mining, which was the core of Tombstone's beginning and its reason for existing, touched many people in many ways. Some of the people who were most directly involved were the men who surveyed and worked in the mines and the assayers evaluating the ore from the mines. Then there were the people who purchased the mines. Apparently the mining bug bit Joseph Stumpf, successful owner of the American Bakery. Perhaps the lure of a possible fortune in his back yard was too much for him to bear. In April, he expanded his interests by leasing the Arizona and Cachise [sic] mines for ninety-nine years at a cost of $100.00.

Another baker in Tombstone had his own ideas about how to earn extra income, but it wasn't the lure of silver that proved profitable for Otto Geisenhofer. Otto boosted his income by supplying meals to the city's prisoners, as Julius Caesar of the NY Bakery and Restaurant did. Otto's earnings must have been good, because he was able to purchase a lot in April near the corner of 8th and Allen Streets that cost $400. The lot was added to his already growing collection of real estate that also included three lots on First Street. Otto had also expanded his bakery to a restaurant earlier in the year. Now patrons could go to the City Bakery and Restaurant to order their favorite meal or baked goods. It seems that Otto's "American" dream was coming true.

American was, not surprisingly, a popular name for businesses in Tombstone and everywhere else, for that matter. One of those businesses was the American Hotel. After dissolving her partnership with Joseph Pascholy and the Russ House on April 6, Nellie Cashman, along with her sister Frances Cunningham, announced that they were opening a new hotel called the American. Situated on 427 and 429 Fremont Street, the new hotel contained a large new dining hall where elegant meals were served at all hours of the day and night. Nellie and "Fannie" would successfully operate this business until the following year.

The Russ House, incidentally, continued to thrive under the management of Joseph Pascholy, thanks to his good sense of business. Committed to running a successful business, Pascholy went to California on a two-week trip. While there, he made arrangements for the Russ House to receive weekly shipments of fresh fish, fruits, and vegetables to insure his patrons had the best.

That spring, Aristotle Petro of the Occidental Chop House announced that he was leaving it. He sold the Occidental to Peter Claudianos earlier in the year, and in April, Peter relocated the restaurant to 5th Street. Mr. Claudianos was fortunate because Alvan Young, who had previously worked as a cook at the chop house, returned. Mr. Young had also been a cook in some of the largest hotels and rotisseries on the Pacific Coast. Fortuitous to find a good cook, Mr. Claudianos was not so lucky when it came to the restaurant's supplies. On the 6th of April, a "dead broke" stole two turkeys from the chop house. Mr. Claudianos reported the theft to the local authorities, and his turkeys, which had been sold to Little Jakey, now at the Pacific Chop House, were promptly returned.

Turkey theft wasn't the only crime committed in town. A man named William Jonry broke into a lodging house and stole several blankets, quilts, pillows, and a mattress. The goods were returned to their rightful owner, and Mr. Jonry spent ninety days in the local jail. In addition to thieves, Tombstone did not look too kindly on anyone using indecent language, as evidenced by the arrest of former assistant district attorney, Frazer. He was arraigned and taken before Judge Wallace in May, whereupon he pled not guilty. At his trial, Frazer was found guilty and fined $39. Since Mr. Frazer was a little short on funds, he was forced to spend some time in jail for his crime until he could raise the money.

A more serious crime was that of assault. Long-time merchant Andrew Cadwell apparently had a sense of humor that equaled his bad temper. On April 9, a young tin apprentice named William Hayes, passed by the store on his way to breakfast. Trying to be funny, Cadwell shoved him off the sidewalk and saying, "Get off you young hoodlum." Hayes returned the push and they got into a scuffle, but when Cadwell got his hat knocked off, he became angry. He reached for a pick and smacked Hayes in the back of his head, leaving him unconscious. Cadwell was promptly arrested and fined. The *Epitaph* also chastised him for losing his temper.

On May 25, the second great fire of Tombstone destroyed four blocks in the business district. This time it was west of 5th Street, the side that the 1881 fire had spared. The flames spread quickly, and the fire showed no mercy in choosing its victims. Even longevity could not save Brown's Hotel, which had been Tombstone's first. The fire quickly demolished most of Tombstone's largest hotels and restaurants including Brown's, Bayley's Restaurant, the Cosmopolitan Hotel, the *Maison Doree* and the Grand Hotel. The *Epitaph* reported that Gus Bilicke had better start rebuilding the Cosmopolitan before the summer rains, or he would have to wait another year. None of them were rebuilt. Charley Brown eventually bought a ranch in the Swisshelm mountains. The Grand's owner, Mrs. McBride, must have been devastated by the fire, especially since she had just lost her husband ten days earlier. The fire was also unfortunate for the proprietors of the *Maison Doree*, who had very recently remodeled the restaurant with all new furnishings, including silver knives, forks, and spoons. Also lost to the fire were the Rockaway Oyster House and Fitzhenry & Mansfield's. These merchants eventually prospered. They purchased the remainder of the lot where their business was located from John Lewellen for $800. Thomas Ward's City Meat Market, which he had recently moved to 511 Allen Street, was also lost. So was Jacob Everhardy's Fremont Street Market. The Occidental Chop House succumbed to the fire, but Mr. Claudianos survived and was able to re-open.

Only three short months after the Campbells had opened their restaurant, the fire destroyed it. The Campbells were persistent people though, and after losing their business, even having no insurance coverage, opened yet another one. At first, the people of Tombstone could find the Campbell's restaurant at 404 Allen Street, but by the end of the year they had moved to 514 Allen Street, which was the former site of the Queen Chop House. The story of the Campbells' triumphs and tragedies demonstrates that it took some hard work, a little optimism, and a great deal of persistence to survive. No matter how many roadblocks the Campbells met, they always seemed to find a new road. Unfortunately, the Campbells eventually met one roadblock they could not get past. On December 1, tragedy struck the Campbells, when Bridget Campbell suddenly became ill with violent spasms and stomach cramps. Dr. Seawell prescribed medicine for her, but the pain did not subside. Another doctor, Dr. Giberson, was called and gave Mrs. Campbell an injection of morphine. A few minutes later, Mrs. Campbell was pronounced dead of poisoning. While the coroner stated she died of natural causes, the *Epitaph* indicated that she might have died of unnatural causes.

Joe Hoefler was an individual whose spirit could not be broken. While the fire may have destroyed his business, he opened his store again, and by the end of 1882, he had another on the corner of 5th and Fremont Streets. Julius and Sophie Caesar also lost their bakery and restaurant to the fire, but were able to re-open by July. Jacob Everhardy re-opened the Fremont Street Market, just opposite of his old location. His new meat market was nestled between the American Hotel and the San Jose House.

Ironically, the month following the fire, the Huachuca Water Works completed its work and distributed water pipes to consumers. Its reservoir had a capacity of 1,100,000 gallons and a pressure so great that water could be thrown 150 feet high. The addition of piped water was said to raise the city's real estate value by fifty percent, and the mining property's value by twenty-five percent. The Tombstone mines also continued to prove profitable by producing rich mineral strikes throughout the year, despite the fire.

Since most of the hotels were consumed by the fire, lodging became a concern for anyone staying in Tombstone. To fill this void, several new lodging houses emerged. One of note was the newly built Palace Lodging House. Run by Mrs. Lucy Young, who formerly owned the Star restaurant, the Palace was said to be the most attractive. The two-story building, located on 5th Street, between Allen and Toughnut, had twenty-five well-ventilated guest rooms, each with a view. The house even had a bathroom on the second floor for the convenience of its guests. Even a fire could not keep Tombstone or its people down; it only forced the town, and those in it, to progress. A month after the fire, Tombstone was almost completely rebuilt and better than before. The San Jose House had been spared from the fire. Mrs. Fallon, now known as Mrs. Z.H. Taylor, had recently designed Tombstone's first-ever conservatory, located in the back of the house. The flower beds were stocked with choice plants tastefully arranged around the sides; the center sported a fountain.

Tasker & Pridham's, which had been spared from the fire, was doing a great business. When Joseph Tasker, one of the owners, was on a trip to Tucson in June, he reported to the *Arizona Daily Star* that the receipts for their merchandise business reached $17,000 per month. His business may have done so well because of the recent fire, which had eliminated some of the competition. With supplies in high demand, their business would almost certainly have increased. A large percentage of the some 5,300 or so inhabitants of Tombstone would have needed a place to shop.

Being a butcher in Tombstone was also quite profitable, at least according to Ernest Storm, who had been a butcher in Tombstone since February 28, 1880. While visiting Tucson in June, he reported to the *Arizona Daily Star* that his company's money receipts amounted to $13,000 per month. Another of Tombstone's long-time butchers, Apollinar Bauer, sold his two lots on Fremont Street where his meat market was located. One of the lots went to the City of Tombstone for $600, the other was sold to O.O. Trantum, a Tombstone attorney, for $700. After selling his lots, he continued to operate his butchering business.

Just as Tombstone's business district recovered from its second devastating fire in May, the threat of another one surfaced in late July. The fire was not as successful as its predecessors had been, mainly because of the new water works in town. The fire started in a back bedroom attached to Mrs. Jones' New Orleans Restaurant, located at the corner of 5th & Toughnut Streets, just opposite from the Russ House. Since the restaurant was constructed of wood, there was not much hope of saving it, or the building next to it. Fortunately for Tombstone, the New Orleans Restaurant was also across from the fire department, which was able to use the pressure of the newly installed water system to suppress the flames that tried to reach other buildings in the city.

Another restaurant on Toughnut Street to disappear rather quickly was the Eureka, but fire was not the reason for its demise. The proprietress was Mrs. Inez McMartin, who opened her restaurant in June and hired James Lane to manage it. He had been in Tombstone since December 12, 1881, and was reportedly the best restaurant man on the Pacific coast. Even though Mrs. McMartin hired the best manager and her bills of fare were bountiful and inexpensive, her restaurant closed in September. McMartin was a shrewd businesswoman, and even more shrewd when it came to deceit. After Mrs. McMartin opened her business, she mortgaged it twice, to two unsuspecting mortgagors. They were Miss Emma Parker, and J.S. McCoy. McCoy was manager of the Huachuca Water Company, and Parker was a woman of somewhat miscellaneous affinities. Neither knew that the other had already mortgaged McMartin's property. McMartin was also indebted to a local butcher for $80. She and her paramour, Joseph Price, a thirty-one-year-old steward, skipped town. They were seen in Benson by Cochise County sheriff, Johnny Behan. At the time, Behan was unaware of the recent dupe committed by McMartin and Price. Upon returning to Tombstone, Behan was advised of the crime, and authorities in Deming, El Paso, and Denver were notified, in an effort to capture the thieves. Unfortunately, the damage was done— Parker was out $300, and McCoy had an uncollectable debt of

$200. To top things off, McMartin had sold her mortgaged property before she left, leaving her creditors no way to collect.

Even with all the town's excitement, Tombstone residents managed to find time in their busy schedules to relax and enjoy themselves throughout the year. In October, the Catholic Church held a fund-raising festival at Schieffelin Hall. The hall had been tastefully decorated for the occasion, and Tombstone's society people turned out in full force to celebrate. They danced to music played by Vincent's band until three o'clock in the morning.

The end of the year seemed to be the time to end and begin partnerships. The firm of Lang, Everhardy & Company ended sometime in 1882, and by December, Jacob Everhardy was back in business on his own at 428 Fremont Street. Of the six butchers listed in *McKenney's Business Directory*, not one consisted of a partnership; they were all operating individually, including Apollinar Bauer. Bauer may have wished he had a partner when Mr. Moberly and Charles Storm paid him a visit in December. The two men entered Bauer's shop and demanded an explanation of certain language Bauer had spoken against them. After a heated discussion, Moberly and Storms drew their pistols, and threatened Bauer's life if he ever spoke against them again. After the two men left, Bauer promptly visited the judge, who swore out a warrant for their arrest. Another partnership change involved George Pridham, of Tasker & Pridham, who sold half of his business interest to Donald A. Macneil for $1,750. The firm was still known as Tasker & Pridham's, though Macneil now owned twenty-five percent of it. Macneil was also part owner of a wholesale grocery store in town with L.W. Carr and H.E. Hills, a former merchant in town who had closed his business in late 1881.

Despite Tombstone's second fire, which destroyed a very populated business district, the city was well on its way to having a good number of newly established businesses. There were approximately six places to stay in Tombstone, including the LeVan Lodging House, the Way Up Lodging House, and the Aztec House. Some of the grocers in town were Cadwell & Stanford's, Frank Austin, Gates & Hickey's, Milich & Dyar's,

Paulina Jones   Silver Lady Antiques

and Fitzhenry & Mansfield's. John Fitzhenry took a break from the business world to attend to some personal business. On September 11, he married Blanche Shakelford of Los Angeles at the private residence of Mr. Davenport. The Fitzhenry's returned to Tombstone, where they intended to reside, and Frank returned to his booming business.

Tombstone's restaurants continued to profit; about seventeen could be found in town. Some of them had already existed, such as the Melrose, though it had new owners—Jane Harding and Catherine Lang. The Russ House continued to prosper, as did the restaurants of Julius Caesar, Robert Campbell, Mrs. Dill, and Walsh & Shanahan. A few of the newer restaurants, and those that rebuilt, included the Grand, Paulina Jones' International Restaurant, Charles Langpaap's restaurant, McCullough

& Tripp's Pacific Chop House, George Modini's restaurant, and Gregory's. The Gregorys had suffered a terrible loss, just one month earlier, when their little boy passed away. Mr. Gregory was also convalescing from a recent illness. The Gregory's were able to pass this sad time in their lives, and remained in Tombstone for several more years.

The Russ House escaped tragedy on December 8, when police officers Solan, Kenney, and Holmes noticed a bright glare coming from the rear of the building. The officers discovered a barrel of hot ashes was dumped and left to burn. They quickly rolled the barrel into the street and extinguished the flames.

Despite the recent tragedies in town, prosperity surrounded Tombstone, and it could be measured by the values of the bullion production for the year of 1882 from the larger mines and mills:

Boston Mill (Custom)	$ 250,000.00
Contention	1,580,542.13
Girard (own & custom ore)	177,540.00
Grand Central	1,358,820.85
Head Center	125,079.81
Knoxville (Stonewall)	1,500,000.00
Tombstone M&M Co.	1,440,895.00
Watervale Mill	15,000.00

The mills in Tombstone were producing, on the average, about $433,155.44 per month, using the above figures. As a result, Tombstone's real estate was becoming a valuable commodity. In 1870, the Territory's total real estate value was assessed at $538,355; in comparison to the 1882 assessment of Tombstone's real estate value alone, which was $917,491.50, one can see just how valuable it was. To say that Tombstone was wealthy would have been an accurate statement.

Tombstone ended the year with prosperous and sophisticated living—successful businesses, productive mines, and even limited telephone service. The most impressive building in Tombstone was also nearly complete. The new courthouse, which was two stories high, constructed of brick, and costing $43,000—was very close to being finished.

Chapter Five
1883

Tombstone
At Its Peak

By the time 1883 arrived Tombstone was a thriving, well-established city that offered resident and visitor alike very comfortable living conditions. There was a hospital, a library, private and public schools, and a newly completed courthouse. For those who sought entertainment, the town had theatres, saloons, gaming rooms, a race track, and a bowling alley. Tombstone continued to offer first-class accommodations and fine dining where tables were supplied with everything the market afforded. The mines were still producing rich quality ore, even though more water began to surface. At first, the water may have presented a problem, but once water pumps were installed and ore was struck below the water level, a greater confidence existed in Tombstone that it would remain a stable place for its 5,000 to 6,000 residents.

After the second fire in 1882, Tombstone's growth continued in an upward trend. Businesses that had been lost to the fire were re-built, and were once again prospering. Even though there were many, already booming businesses in town, more new ones opened, but not on the scale of previous years. Tombstone's business district continued to be an ever-changing one where people came and went. Some opened their own businesses, while other newcomers bought existing establishments—the case with the Grand Restaurant. As the year began, the owner sold its entire contents. Seth M. Owens sold the chairs, tables, curtains, mirrors, table linens, chandeliers, and everything else that could be removed, to Frank N. Wolcott for $1,200. The Grand, itself, would soon have a new owner, too.

Frank Wolcott was the manager of Woodhead & Gay's Cash Store, but would soon be the proprietor of his own business, one that would last until after the turn of the century. Whether Frank bought the items from the Grand to furnish his new store or to sell as merchandise is unknown. Regardless of what he did with his purchases, he opened his grocery and provision store on 5th Street, between Allen and Fremont. His business location doubled as his residence, as it did for many of Tombstone's business people. After Frank opened his store, he hired Thomas Allison as salesman and DeWitt Messick as clerk. Messick later became Wolcott's business partner.

One business that did not change owners was the Fremont Street Market, owned by Jacob Everhardy, who employed his brother, Matthew, and Anton Louch. James Carruthers was another Tombstone butcher who remained in operation; he employed C.F. Hill and William Kellog. The butcher moved his business to Thomas Ward's old butcher stand on Allen Street, between 5th and 6th Streets. The Can Can was another well-established business that was operated by its original owners. Andrew Walsh and William Shanahan continued to operate the Can Can successfully, and in June reported to the city clerk that their business would not exceed $5,000 per month. This was done to keep their business license at a certain rate. If they exceeded the $5,000 limit, their business license cost would increase. With their business booming, they hired Henry Haninger, Charles Wilson, and Thomas Wren as waiters to serve the meals that were prepared by cook Henry Holthower. Holthower was previously in the restaurant business when he leased the Grand Hotel Dining Room in late 1881.

The Rockaway Oyster House had been re-built and was still going strong, but under the new name of the Rockaway Restaurant. The Rockaway continued to operate under the skillful ownership of John Bogovich & Company. The persistent and hard-working Robert Campbell remained in the restaurant busi-

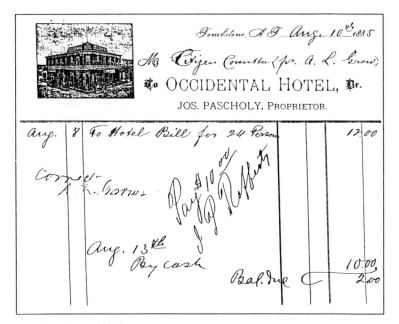

Occidental Hotel bill   Arizona Historical Society

ness, too. Because Paulina Jones' New Orleans Restaurant was destroyed in a fire, and she did not re-open it, Robert changed his current restaurant name, St. Louis, back to its first name, New Orleans. He also announced that he was back at his old location on 4th Street once again.

One of the few new eating establishments to open that year, was the California Restaurant, at 715 Allen Street. Sophie Gregor was the owner. To solicit new business, she placed an ad in the *Tombstone Republican* that read, "Wanted. Seventy-five able bodied men to board at the California Restaurant."

The mercantile store, Fitzhenry & Mansfield's, was still in business and remained popular in town, as did Tasker & Pridham's, which employed Edward J. Swift. Earlier in the year, Swift invented "Swift's Water Reducer." The water reducer was designed to confine water flowing through a faucet into a smaller space. It is not know whether his patent was granted or not. Tasker and Pridham purchased a portion of a lot at the corner of 3rd and Allen Streets at a cost of $300. Shortly after the purchase,

George Pridham, Donald A. Macneil, and Frank Lester Moore bought a portion of Joseph Tasker's business interest for $1, as he planned to leave Tombstone. These merchants, as well as others, always received a variety of imported goods from all across the U.S. and various foreign countries. Goods were shipped to commission merchants, like Joseph Goldwater by way of the great American rail system. Goldwater's office was in Fairbank, where the railroad made a stop. From there, he and others delivered merchandise to businesses in Tombstone. Merchants, in turn, offered them to the public and other businesses.

The *Maison Doree*, associated with the Cosmopolitan Hotel, had been destroyed in Tombstone's second fire, but another *Maison Doree* opened in town. The new one, situated on 5th Street between Allen and Fremont Streets, was owned by Steve DeMartini, who employed George Mandich. Steve advertised the *Maison Doree* Rotisserie's specialty was Italian dishes, including ravioli.

Probably the finest hotel to be seen in town after the destruction of the Cosmopolitan, Brown's, and the Grand, was the Occidental Hotel, which was opened in 1883 by Joseph Pascholy and Godfried Tribolet, at the corner of 4th and Allen Streets. This new hotel was rather large and covered five lots on Allen Street and could easily accommodate 100 guests. Pascholy and Tribolet hired Louis Souc as clerk to check their guests in, Gus Westcamp as porter to assist with their bags, and Mary Tack as housekeeper to maintain the high-class standards that would soon become the hallmark of the Occidental. The hotel also had a first-class restaurant, appropriately named the Occidental Restaurant. This restaurant was not associated with Aristotle Petro's of the same name that had once served Tombstone elegant French meals. It had gone out of business earlier in the year. Jennie Harden, who once owned the Boss Restaurant at 605 Allen Street, ran the new Occidental Restaurant. She had sold the restaurant to Miss Long, who hired Sallie Fletcher to work for her at the Boss.

On July 6, Tombstone weathered the effects of a cyclone. It was reported that the cyclone was the most violent storm Tomb-

Ad for Russ House   McKenney's 1882 Business Directory

stone had ever witnessed. It filled the air with debris and huge clouds of dust. Many outbuildings were ripped down. As the wind slowly died down, hail, wind, lightning, and rain pounded the city, for about an hour. This was followed by gentle rain that fell upon Tombstone. There were a few structural casualties, but no one was seriously injured. The porch of the San Jose House was torn down and rested on the sidewalk. The cellar of City Hall was flooded, and the signs on the O.K. Corral and the Occidental Restaurant were carried away.

Before opening the Occidental, Joseph Pascholy had been the proprietor of the Russ House, located at the corner of 5th and Toughnut Streets. Pascholy left the Russ House in very capable hands. It was once again under the careful and successful management of Miss Nellie Cashman, along with her sister, Frances "Fannie" Cunninghman. The Russ House remained a very popular hotel, and to ensure that their guests were well-taken care of, the sisters employed the following people: Sol Anderson, barkeeper and former owner; Alex Bacilli, pantryman; Charles

Territory of Arizona } ss.
County of Cochise }

Pauline Streckenbach being first duly sworn deposes and says that she is a widow, and is carrying on business on her own account in the "Grand Restaurant" on Allen Street, between 4th and 5th Streets in the City of Tombstone, Arizona Territory.

Subscribed and sworn to before me this 23rd day of October A.D. 1883

P. Streckenbach.

A.J. Felter
Justice of the Peace

Affidavit from Pauline Streckenbach, owner of the Grand Restaurant
Arizona Historical Society

Blair, waiter; and Harry Miller, steward. The Russ House, under the management of Nellie and Fannie, remained one of the most popular places to eat and room in Tombstone.

Another popular place to dine in Tombstone was the Grand Restaurant on Allen Street. The old favorite had acquired yet another new owner—Mrs. Pauline Streckenbach. Since the Grand's contents had been sold earlier in the year, her first priority was to procure furnishings for her new business. While she managed the restaurant, Armand Tuquet prepared elegant French meals for the Grand's patrons.

Tombstone now averaged fifteen restaurants and eating houses—about the same number as in the two previous years. Many of them were old favorites, while others were new. Many of Tombstone's residents were involved in the restaurant business, either as owner or as employees. A stroll down the streets of Tombstone allowed patrons to choose their favorite restaurant and meet the people who made them popular. The American Restaurant was owned Mrs. S.J. Dill, who employed J. Williams to assist her. Mrs. Dill also prepared meals for the city's prisoners. At the Brooklyn Restaurant, owned by Joseph A. Bright, was a waitress named Katie Lacy. Mrs. Maggie McGivney, the head cook, prepared meals. Gregory's was owned by Thomas Gregory, who employed Louis Albright as its cook, and the American House was owned by Mrs. H.E. Hanford, who employed Mrs. Love as her housekeeper. Paulina Jones owned the International Restaurant, and employed Katy Rafferty, Louise Rollins, and Belle Perry. Jeannie Harding and Catherine Lang remained the proprietresses of the Melrose Restaurant. These ladies employed E.B. Lang, who worked behind the scenes to keep their books in order, and Lizzie McCormick to wait on customers and keep the dining room running smoothly. Otto Geisenhofer's City Bakery and restaurant was now located at 513 Allen Street, and just down the street from his old bakery location. Julius Caesar moved his New York Restaurant to Otto's old location on Allen Street, between 5th and 6th Streets. Another of Tombstone's restaurants was the Pacific Chop House, owned by John McCullough, who employed E.T. Newett and George Walker to wait on customers.

Butcher shops also served as a source of employment. Many of Tombstone's first butchers remained in business, including Ernest Storm, Charles Bacigalupi, and Robert Clifford, who employed George Wambach. One of the new butcher shops was owned by the Prout brothers who operated their business on Allen Street, between 6th and 7th. Mr. Tinklee, John Murphy, Ryan Murnane, and John McGarvin owned the others. Apollinar Bauer was still in business, but an event earlier in the year had nearly changed that. He was arrested for selling diseased meat on a warrant sworn out by two of his employees. They claimed that

Tombstone
Oct. 31st 1884

The City of Tombstone
Dr. to Mrs Dill

To boarding City prisoners for the months
of September And October as follows: to wit,
Meals given before you required me to item
ize my bills, twenty Seven in the month
of September ————————— 27

Meals given to Tierachmianano (23 days) 46
" " Ah John (30 days) 60

October Month
Meals to Wm Allen , , , 4
" J. S. Fountain , , , 2
" Neal Devine , , , 10
" Jesus Hirara , , , 10
" — Maloney , , , 2
" Jack O'Brien , , , 8
" Neal Devine , , , 3
" Charly Barr , , , 2
" Neal Devine 3

Meals Total number 177
Total amount for the two months $44.25.

I hereby Certify that the foregoing bill is true And Correct And
that no part thereof has heritofore been presented or paid,

Jas Boyle
Chief of Police

Bill to city for prisoners' meals from Mrs. Dill   Arizona Historical Society

some sheep died on Bauer's ranch, and he had them skinned and soaked to be sold at his market. Apollinar was later cleared of the charges and went on to prosper.

The grocery stores were another place to find employment. Tasker, Pridham & Company, employed John Montz as their warehouseman, and M.E. Shaffner, along with Ed Swift, as their clerks to assist the customers with their purchases. Cadwell & Stanford's grocery store, one of Tombstone's first, remained in business; Charles Wiser was their clerk. Pascal M. Dyar was a partner in the new merchant store of Dyar, Finch & Baldwin. He was also a partner in the grocery store known as Milich & Dyar. P.W. Smith was still dealing in general merchandise and was also president of the Cochise County Bank. Joseph Hoefler continued to be a competitor in the grocery store business and employed Louis Himebrich as clerk to assist his customers with their purchases.

For fresh baked goods or ice cream, residents visited the many bakeries in town, such as the American Bakery owned by Joseph Stumpf, the French Bakery at 628 Fremont Street, or Mr. Langpaap's bakery at 515 Fremont Street. The Eclipse Bakery was another aromatic place to make purchases; it was owned by J.M. Nash who employed Daniel Harley and L.H. Nash was the bakery's driver delivering daily fresh baked goods. Close to the post office, was the temptation of Frank Yaple's ice cream parlor, where customers could sample some of his ice cream or freshly made candy.

Planning for his children's future, Joseph Stumpf purchased a lot on 4th Street for $800, which was held in trust for his children, Emma, Franco, and Joseph, Jr. For a break from the summer heat, the children could visit the town's new built swimming pool. Not just a hole in the ground, the pool had a cover, its own bar, and changing rooms. Admission to the pool was fifty cents, the same cost of a complete meal at one of Tombstone's finer restaurants.

The fact that people were investing in their future, and their children's, was a good indication that Tombstone would continue to prosper. As testimony to this, Tombstone residents began planting trees and flower gardens to beautify their homes and businesses. Unbeknownst to its 6,300 residents, however, Tombstone and its mines had already reached their peak. Who would have thought that a town with a new courthouse and city hall, good hotels, numerous restaurants, several newspapers, and two stable banks would ever fail? Even the merchants in town were reporting monthly sales in excess of $250,000. But, mining is a risky and unpredictable industry that determines the success or failure of those with whom it associates. The only person who may have known what the future held was Madame Ralph, Tombstone's fortune teller.

CHAPTER SIX
1884-1889

DOWNWARD SLOPE

By 1884, Tombstone was considered the greatest "mining camp" in the territory. Even though mining was the genesis of Tombstone and continued to support it, its residents took offense at being called a "mining camp." After all, its mines were producing ore that amounted to about $500,000 per month and could hardly be called a "camp" anymore. The city of Tombstone was flourishing, and continued to do so in a year that looked very promising. The public school alone employed five teachers and averaged about 250 students in attendance on any given school day. The banks in town remained stable and the Cochise County Bank maintained a capital of $150,000. The personal property values also continued to grow and now exceeded $1,500,000. The evidence would have made anyone feel secure in Tombstone's future, and that is why the food businesses, as well as many others, remained successful.

Even though Tombstone was fairly stable, its residents were always on the move. It is doubtful that one could dine in a restaurant in 1883 and go back the following year to find the same owner, or cook for that matter. For one, Armand Tuquet was no longer preparing the meals at the Grand Restaurant because he was now the proud owner of the *Maison Doree*.

Long-time merchant Frank Wolcott remained in business, but on February 1, he initiated a new policy of strictly selling for cash at his grocery store. This new policy enabled him to offer his customers a better rate on their purchases since he no longer needed to mark up his prices to cover unpaid debts. Later that year, Frank purchased two lots on Fitch Street, which likely served as his residence.

The grocery store business continued to be a profitable venture, as well as a competitive one. The established merchants Fitzhenry and Mansfield advertised that "they lead them all." The advertisements even implied that if customers wanted the best, they should patronize Fitzhenry & Mansfield's. Here is a sample of how and what they advertised:

- For the sweetest and best hams and bacon go to Fitzhenry & Mansfield's.
- Our "gilt edge" butter cannot be surpassed.

Another ad stated, "In spite of precautions taken by the government it is an established fact that teas are adulterated with coloring matter in New York, after passing government inspections. Fitzhenry & Mansfield's Treasure Tea defies adulteration or mixing, as the customers get it in Perfection tea cans, sealed by the shippers in Japan."

The other large mercantile firm, Tasker, Pridham & Company, became known as Pridham, Macneil & Moore's when Joseph Tasker left the business and Tombstone a few months earlier. Tasker eventually ended up in Soldier's Hole in the Sulphur Spring valley, where he "kept the station" for a couple of years. Pridham, Macneil & Moore's, like Fitzhenry & Mansfield's, was determined to be the most popular merchant in town. Advertisements stated it was the family grocery store and would supply boarding houses, restaurants, and families at "bed-rock" prices. While shopping at Pridham, Macneil & Moore's for Los Gatos flour, sugar cured hams, and Budweiser beer, patrons could also pick up some high explosives, since the store advertised the best and cheapest of the age.

In June, Nellie Cashman sold the personal property in the Russ House to her sister Fannie Cunningham and Kate Ward for $3,500. It would appear that Nellie was quite a good businesswoman who kept a well-stocked pantry. The following items are only a partial list of what was sold:

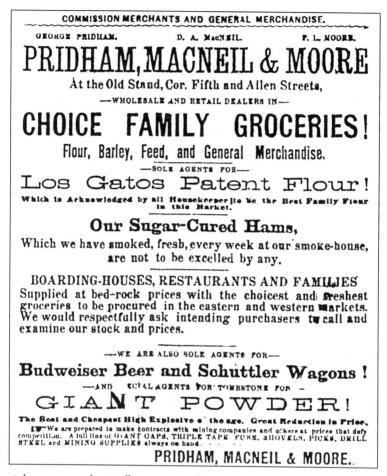

Advertisement for Pridham, Macneil & Moore   Tombstone Epitaph, 1884

6 cases oysters	4 1/2 dozen squash
8 dozen salmon	1 sack salt
1 case coconut cakes	200 lbs. lard
15 gallons port wine	40 lbs. dried raisins
4 barrels beer	100 lbs. rice
1/2 barrel vinegar	20 dozen whiskey
8 gallons catsup	8 dozen grapes
2 1/2 barrels mackerel	500 lbs. dried apples
60 lbs. dried corn	7 gallons brandy
2 barrels blackberry brandy	500 lbs. ham

Some of the other items included in the transaction were flavoring extracts, macaroni, yeast, canned pie fruits, and spices. Nellie would have purchased these goods from the merchants in town, as well as ordering directly from the companies themselves. There were also a variety of non-food items, some of which were cots, pillows, mirrors, utensils and the ever necessary spittoons. Why Nellie completed this transaction is not clearly known. The indication was that she might have been attempting to set her sister up in business. Unfortunately for Fannie, she would not live through the year to see the benefit of her purchases because she succumbed to tuberculosis. When Nellie lost her sister, she gained the responsibility of Fannie's five young children to raise, along with a very large business to manage by herself. This did not hinder Nellie though, and she continued be a good business-woman who was an upstanding and involved member of her community.

The entire community was seriously affected when the Hudson & Company Bank failed in May. The bank's failure was largely due to overspeculation in land development in Tucson. While the county was able to withdraw $30,000 from the bank before it closed its doors, the miners and townspeople were not. Because the bank's deposits were not insured, as they are today, many people lost whatever savings they had deposited.

Another significant event to take place in 1884, was a serious labor dispute that temporarily stopped Tombstone's mining operation. A large portion of the men in Miner's Union agreed to strike until the working conditions and wages were improved. The dispute was eventually settled and the men returned to the mines. The miner's strike may have been influenced by the recent bank failure. Nonetheless, Tombstone and its people put these two major events behind them and moved forward. Tombstone ended 1884 and began 1885 ready to embrace yet another year of productive mining and prosperous living.

The new year began with new legislation. On February 27, 1885, the Territory of Arizona's Legislature enacted a more definitive law for the protection of livestock growers. This new act included regulations the previous act had set forth, but also defined new ones. Three changes directly affected the butchers operating in the Arizona Territory. The first one dealt with the $1,000 bond. Not only did a butcher have to file a bond, he was required to have at least one good and sufficient surety besides himself file a $1,000 bond. The second change required a butcher, if he owned cattle, to register his brand and/or mark to be kept on file with the county in which he resided. The final change was about keeping the animal's hide for inspection. Instead of keeping only the hide, the butcher had to retain the hide with the ears attached. The purpose was so the brand on the hide, as well as the owner's mark on the ear, could identify the animal.

Apollinar Bauer did not waste time in filing his $1,000 bond—he filed in March with Cochise County. Also in keeping with the law, he had a surety, in his case two, file a bond for him. Joseph Stumpf, owner of the American Bakery, and Les Summerfield, owner of Summerfield Dry Goods, each put up $500. A few months later Apollinar joined C.S. Abbott, another one of Tombstone's pioneer butchers who had formerly owned the California Market, and J.R. Bradley, to form the Tombstone Wholesale Butcher Company. Shortly after they formed this company, they took in two partners named Sigfried and Abraham Tribolet who purchased a one-quarter interest in the company for $1,400. The Tribolet brothers were already well established businessmen in the community and had previously owned the Eagle Market butcher shop.

Not only butchers were affected by a changing atmosphere. The Can Can Restaurant, which had been in business for five years, hired two veteran restaurant men from California. Benjamin Wurtmann, former chief cook at the Pacific Ocean House in Santa Cruz, prepared the meals at the Can Can, while his former co-worker at San Francisco's Popular Restaurant, Mr. Woodward, was the steward. Wurtmann was only with the Can Can for a short time. Later in the year, he would be cooking meals at the Russ House for Nellie Cashman. The Can Can's former cook, Henry Holthower, left Tombstone for Aspen, Colorado, which was being touted as the next "Tombstone." A few months after Henry left, he wrote to his old Tombstone friends that Aspen was crowded and overdone. He also claimed that nine out of ten miners were broke, and advised his friends to stay in town, as they were far better off.

Some of Tombstone's other original restaurants were experiencing change, too. The Star Restaurant, owned by Mrs. Paddock-Doyle, would soon have a new owner, Mrs. Brockman. The New York Restaurant, Bakery and Coffee House closed because its owners, Julius and Sophie Caesar, purchased a half interest in the Crystal Palace Saloon for $2,500. Ben Wehrfritz had been the sole owner of the Crystal Palace since his former partner, Sigfried Tribolet, left to start his own brewery. When their partnership dissolved in 1882, Sigfried took the Golden Eagle Brewery name with him. Ben's brewery became the Crystal Palace. With their investment, Julius and Sophie Caesar, formerly restaurateurs, were now part owners of the Crystal Palace Saloon. Next, the Caesar's leased a lot on Allen Street, between 2nd and 3rd Streets, from the Vizina Mining Company for ninety-nine years, at a cost of $300.

The grocers, Fitzhenry and Mansfield, had a rather unpleasant incident take place on May 23 of this year. To begin with, the store's safe was robbed. As if their loss was not bad enough, Fitzhenry and Mansfield had to listen to allegations that they, or one of the two of them, knew more about the robbery than they cared to tell. Finally in September, the perpetrator, W. H. Smith, was convicted of grand larceny, which helped to exonerate the owners. Smith had two accomplices, Charles Blair, former owner of the Way Up Lodging House, and one of his porters. Blair was released due to lack of evidence. With this unpleasantness behind them, Fitzhenry & Mansfield's continued to fill the newspapers with ads for a variety of goods. It is interesting, though, that by the end of the year, John Fitzhenry had left the business and Tombstone as well. Regardless of Fitzhenry's reasons for leaving, his business partner, Russel Mansfield, remained in town. He continued to offer Tombstone a variety of goods, including the usual fine selection of teas and coffees, as well as pure maple syrup.

GROCERIES
AND
PROVISIONS.

The Choicest of Dried Meats and fish
of all kinds and at reasonable
rates; also a choice line of

Family Groceries,
Fresh Ranch Butter and Eggs,
Fresh Fruit, Berries and
Garden Vegetables
At Lowest Cash Prices
312 ALLEN STREET 312
Wm. Head,   Proprietor,
☞ Branch Eclipse Bakery,

Advertisement for William Head   Tombstone Epitaph, 1885

Another merchant advertised in competition with Fitzhenry
& Mansfield's. His ad appeared adjacent to theirs. William Head
promoted his Family Grocery store at 312 Allen Street. Mr.
Head advertised that fresh ranch butter, eggs, berries, and garden
vegetables were available at the lowest cash prices. Butter was a
valuable commodity, but recently the fear that some butters were
not the genuine article, began to surface. The fear was not of
Tombstone merchants tampering with it, but other merchants
in Tucson or Prescott. The *Epitaph* described how to test butter
to see if it was pure. One could put a few drops of sulfuric acid
on cream butter, and if it turned pure white, was real. If the butter

were artificially colored yellow, it would turn dark red. Animal or vegetable fat used to manufacture "butter" would give it a rainbow color. Being a profitable merchant in town was proving to be a matter of reputation. Even though William Head was now a grocer in town, he had previously worked as a carpenter in 1881 and as a miner in Russell City in 1882.

Grocery store merchants were not the only ones to advertise at this time. Browsing through the *Daily Tombstone* newspaper, one would have found an ad for Mrs. Holland's California Restaurant, as well as Jacob Everhardy's Fremont Street Meat Market, Joseph Stumpf's American Bakery, Paulina Jones' International Restaurant, and Freeman and Coleman's Pacific Chop House. Shortly after their ad appeared, they dissolved their partnership and the Pacific Chop House closed. The Melrose Restaurant was no longer placing ads or serving meals, for that matter, but its location was still being used by the Natural Ice Company, where F.C. Hawkins sold ice at three cents per pound and offered free delivery.

Mr. Hawkins was not the only one to sell ice in town; he had competition from Julius Caesar and Ben Wehrfritz, co-owners of the Crystal Palace Saloon. They were offering ice at two and one-half cents per pound and announced they kept a large supply constantly on hand with no danger of selling out, but they did not mention free delivery. Hawkins left Tombstone in September for Denver, Colorado. He joined Isaac "Little Jakey" Jacobs, a former restaurant man in town, to open an "elegant" restaurant in Denver.

There were many businesses in town that offered free delivery, but commission merchants did not. Charging for delivery of goods was their whole purpose for being, and that is why George Buford, after trying his hand at mining, became a commission merchant. Buford, like Joseph Goldwater, was located in Fairbank, the town to which many of the goods were delivered by train. He advertised that he would attend to the hauling of freight from Fairbank to Tombstone. He stated that freight orders to be delivered, should be left with Tombstone merchants, Macneil, Moore & Company; Wolcott & Messick; Dyar, Finch & Baldwin's; Frank Austin; or McAllister & McCone.

For reasons unknown, long-time merchants Cadwell and Stanford decided to leave Tombstone. Could it have been that these merchants, who had arrived in Tombstone before it began to peak, also had the insight to leave before it hit rock bottom? Perhaps they did, or maybe they were just lucky; only they and their associates knew the actual reasons for their departure. Once decided, they placed an ad in the *Daily Record Epitaph* asking anyone who owed them money to settle with them at once to avoid legal action.

While Cadwell and Stanford closed their business, Harry Wisdom opened his. He announced that the Fountain Restaurant on Allen Street had been renovated, painted and thoroughly refitted. He boasted that it was one of the "neatest places in town to get a meal," and stated that fresh pumpernickel bread would be served daily to his patrons. The Fountain offered its patrons a good variety of breakfast, lunch, and dinner entrees to choose from, including rock cod, tom cod, sea bass, and Spanish mackerel. The fish served for breakfast at the Fountain had been packed in ice and shipped by express from California. The owners also tempted diners by claiming their restaurant was the coolest place in town to have a meal because there was no smoke, heat, or smell from the kitchen, which was entirely separate from the dining room. They served their customers nothing but the choicest cuts of beef, fish, game, and oysters, along with steaks, cutlets, chops, ranch eggs, and buttermilk.

Under the ownership of Armand and Amelia Tuquet, the *Maison Doree* was not as successful as it had once been. The chef Armand hired was not pleasing the public, and in September, Armand announced that he would be cooking again. Armand also relied on his French friend, Dan Ieuch, to manage the dining room. The *Daily Record Epitaph* acknowledged this by placing a "Notice to the Public" in their September 18 issue. The notice stated that Armand, a French cook, had taken charge of his kitchen and would be doing his own cooking, which was sure to please everyone. Armand also applied for a membership in the Ancient Order of United Workmen (A.O.U.W.). The application contained some very unusual information. First, Armand stated he weighed 165 pounds and was five feet, two inches tall. He claimed he resembled his mother, and that she died when she was fifty-eight during her change of life. He also said his father died at sixty-two from old age! He stated he used tobacco ten times daily and did not use opium. Armand also referenced, Joseph Pascholy, as a close and intimate friend. When asked about wine, he noted he "used" two bottles of Claret wine daily, but did not drink to excess. It is not know whether his membership was approved or declined.

Pascholy's Occidental Hotel was still booming, and was the latest scene of a good old-fashioned brawl. It seems that waiter, Harry Miller, and porter, Fred Hall were discussing the safe robbing that took place at Fitzhenry & Mansfield's. Hall was a principal witness against the accused, while Miller was a personal friend of his. Miller was said to be the aggressor of the fight, and Hall was the victor. Before the two did damage to the hotel, officer Holmes arrested Miller and threw him in jail. He then returned to the hotel, and secured Hall. Hall made bail with the help of his employer, Joseph Pascholy, while Miller remained in jail overnight to cool off.

Tombstone was a town with a variety of entertainment. Performances were held at the local halls and theatres, there was gambling, and there were many private parties. On one late summer afternoon, a Tombstone couple named Mr. and Mrs. Springer, had a birthday party for their little Edna. The festivities at the party included card playing, music, dancing, and a large lunch spread. Although some of the mines had been shut down, the year of 1885 ended optimistically. This feeling could have been attributed to the mines that remained in operation, which, with the help of water pumps, continued to generate enough ore that allowed most businesses to remain in operation.

The next year was a decidedly disappointing one for Tombstone. Most of the mines would shut down due to flooding. It's ironic to think that water, something so precious in Tombstone, is what eventually ended an era of high living that would never again be achieved in Tombstone. However, the era was not over yet, and the people of Tombstone were determined to continue making a living in the mining town they called home.

Apollinar Bauer, a Tombstone pioneer, was one of the people who still called Tombstone home. He continued in the butchering business, along with his partners, J.R. Bradley and Sigfried Tribolet. At some point, Apollinar and his partners acquired a slaughterhouse that had once been owned by Washington Coffee and Thomas Ward, both earlier Tombstone butchers. The slaughterhouse was located two miles from town on the lower road to Charleston. In March, Bauer, Bradley, and Tribolet sold it for $2,500 to Ernest Storm, another Tombstone butcher, and John Slaughter, the town's sheriff. Included in the sale were the stables, sheds, four horses, three wagons, and the property known as Abbott's Spring, plus a sheep corral that was about one and one-half miles southwest of the slaughterhouse. It is interesting to note that Thomas Ward purchased this ranch in 1879 for $3,000. Could this have been an indication that property values in and around Tombstone were declining?

Since Tombstone's early days, there had been a large Chinese population. Some of them owned businesses in town, and many of them held a variety of jobs in the community including launderers and cooks. Unfortunately, there had been a movement to push all the Chinese out of Tombstone. An advertisement was placed by the Pacific Chop House that read, "The Chinese must go!" The ad continued, "...on March 1st, the Chinese now employed in the Pacific Chop House must go. D.J. Carter will assume control of the culinary department and W.L. Fenton will have charge of the dining room..." This was just one of the many ways that the Chinese were forced out of Tombstone.

Many residents and business owners were determined to stay. People like Otto Geisenhofer, the first man to establish a bakery in town, still wanted to call Tombstone home. While Otto was set on remaining in town, he did not put all his proverbial eggs in one basket. He not only owned a bakery and restaurant in Tombstone, but he had opened a bakery in San Leandro, California called the San Leandro Bakery. He also set up his brother Michael in his own business in San Leandro called the

Otto Geisenhofer photograph from Fly's Gallery

German Bakery and Coffee Saloon. When Otto was in California, he stayed with his brother in the six bedroom house he had built for Michael. Even though Otto frequently traveled to San Leandro, his primary residence was Tombstone, and when he was in Tombstone, his brother ran both California businesses.

California continued to be a primary resource for the merchandise arriving in Tombstone, and the town's merchants were quick to advertise what would be arriving. Russel Mansfield advertised he had received fresh cranberries, and Joe Hoefler announced that Louisiana molasses was available for $1.25 a gallon. Dyar & Baldwin's was selling fine Sonora oranges at thirty-five cents a dozen, while Messick and Wolcott were offering a "choice lot" of dried fruit, eastern oatmeal, hominy, dried beef, and Pioneer Mills flour, along with comb and extract honey. Although grocers sold milk, it was not fresh; it was usually condensed. Those wanting fresh milk could purchase it from Abbott & Peck's dairy farm just outside of town. What a luxury this must have been to the people of Tombstone!

Nellie Cashman, a Tombstone veteran, decided to move to Nogales, Arizona Territory. She did not go alone; Paulina Jones who owned the International Restaurant joined her. The two left Tombstone, and each had plans to open their own hotel and restaurant in Nogales. Nellie's Russ House was now under the proprietorship of Mrs. T. S. O'Brien, and Ben Wurtmann, who was the chief cook, prepared its meals. Later in the year, Mary O'Brien left the Russ House to open the Arcade Restaurant at Cadwell & Stanford's former location. When this happened, Nellie Cashman was back in Tombstone and took charge of the Russ House.

It was business as usual for Tombstone. The mines continued to generate ore with the help of water pumps. Then suddenly, in May, a fire burned the mine pumps, and the mines began to flood with water again. As a result, very little mining continued, and the people living in Tombstone started to close their businesses. Although a few previously left, the emigration was on a much larger scale now. While many people left Tombstone for parts unknown, some remained in hope that the mines would again begin to produce on the scale that they once had. Unfortunately, large scale mining never returned to Tombstone and its population continued to decrease.

Julius and Sophie Caesar must have thought that Tombstone had a chance, because they stayed. They did, however, lease the Crystal Palace, and they sold its contents to William H. Curnow, who was a former Tombstone miner, for $600. The sale, which took place in June, included barrels of whiskey, gin, sherry, champagne, a piano, and a counter music box. Even though the Caesars sold the business to Curnow, they retained ownership of the land and a storage room in the back of the Crystal Palace for making beer.

The fact that many people were leaving Tombstone and selling their property showed the uncertainty they felt about the town's future in 1886. This was certainly understandable since it was the mines that had made Tombstone the prosperous city they had known.

By the time 1887 had arrived, only a couple of mines were still operating on a small scale. The town's businesses remained in operation, but their numbers were shrinking. Tombstone's earliest residents ran a majority of the businesses that remained in operation. Perhaps these pioneers were determined to survive in Tombstone because of the amount of time and money they had already invested in it. Their continuing operation could have been due to the lack of competition because very few new businesses, or people for that matter, came to Tombstone. Some of the businesses may have seemed new because their names had changed, but they were still being owned and operated by people who had been in Tombstone from its earliest years. Many business owners diversified to attract a wider retail market.

One of the pioneers was merchant Joe Hoefler, who had changed the name of his business to the Pioneer Store. He still carried a variety of general merchandise, but now specialized in agricultural supplies for ranchers and supplies for miners. Frank Wolcott was still in town supplying people with groceries like fresh ranch butter, fresh fish, and Eastern oysters every Thursday. The newspaper advertised large quantities of freight were still arriving in town and would be available to the public. Items such as wine, liquors, various food products, cigars, toiletries, and clothing were included in these shipments. Other imported goods, such as French peas, Italian mushrooms, olive oil from Tuscany, and Swiss cheese could be purchased from the Old French Market at the corner of Allen and 6th Streets. Another merchant, Emil Sydow, had come to Tombstone a little later than most, but still remained. He advertised that $1 could buy any of the following:

5 lbs. good Japan Tea	10 lbs. salt pork
12 lbs. good coffee sugar	5 cans jams or jellies
25 bars Housekeeper's Soap	6 bottles California wine

A large freight shipment arrived in Tombstone carrying two-year-old fruit trees such as peach, pear, apple, and persimmon. The shipment also included grape vines, carnations, twenty-two varieties of roses, and other assorted plants. The people who remained in Tombstone were determined to make their city a beautiful place to live, regardless of the size of the town's population. Entertainment also made Tombstone a pleasant place to live, including festivals and parties, like the St. Patrick's Ball that was held on March 17.

Unfortunately, the night before St. Patrick's day, Edward Swift, a former employee of Pridham, Macneil & Moore's, got into a fight with Jerry Barton over an unpaid liquor bill. Jerry claimed that Edward owed him money from a party of firemen who had been in his saloon in Benson. The men exchanged heated words and fists flew which resulted in Edward being knocked down, and Barton being taken before the City Recorder who fined him $8. Sadly, it was not the end of the fight, because later in the evening Barton and Swift ran into to each other again. Although no one knew how the second fight started, everyone was aware of the outcome. Barton grabbed Swift, who was slightly over sixty years old, by the beard and punched him about the face and neck two or three times then threw him to the ground. Bystanders who witnessed the end of the fight picked up Swift's lifeless body and carried it into his former employer's store. They tried to resuscitate him, but their efforts were in vain because he had died almost immediately from a broken neck. Swift's funeral was held the following day at the firehouse of Engine Co. No. 1 where he had been one of their oldest members. He was survived by a wife and several grown children. A few days after the funeral it was reported that Swift's wife was in a precarious condition and in need of food. One could only hope that the townspeople came to her rescue. One of the Tribolet's, Chief Fire Engineer, and a close associate of Ed Swift's, may have led the cause.

The Tribolets had been some of the first people to start operating a butchering business in Tombstone and they continued to be a force throughout the years. Sigfried and Abraham had become partners in the Tombstone Wholesale Butcher Company and now Sigfried was the proprietor of the Union Meat Market. The market was located on Allen Street, between 6th and 7th Streets. Sigfried sold any kind of desired beef, pork, mutton, sausages, salt pork, leaf lard, head cheese, and bologna sausages. He also advertised discounts for cash purchases. Even the butchers were leery of selling on credit. One could hardly blame them, with the instability that surrounded Tombstone.

With the future of Tombstone uncertain, a large number of people began to panic and physically removed their homes from the city. So in April, the Mayor and Common Council of Tombstone passed a law that prohibited houses and/or buildings from being removed from town. The new ordinance, #60, secured the protection of property within the city limits. It prohibited anyone from removing a frame building, dwelling, cabin, or other structure without first obtaining a permit from the Mayor or a member of the council. The permit had to be countersigned by the Chief of Police. Anyone found guilty of violating the ordinance was convicted of a misdemeanor, fined between $30 and $50, and/or imprisoned for a maximum of thirty days.

Tombstone's real estate market was in trouble. The value of the property had dramatically dropped. Tombstone's city assessor, G.W. Chapman, announced the real estate and personal property assessments totaled $507,506, which was more than a fifty percent decrease from just four years earlier. With the real estate and property values dropping, rumors began to spread. One rumor was that the Girard Mill would join the other the mines and shut down on May 1. The mill's superintendent attempted to quell that fear by stating "the mill will run just so long as it can get water supply, and at present I know of no probability of such a thing happening as a failure in water. Of course it is among the possibilities." Eventually water became a problem for the Girard Mill, and the other mines still operating in the area.

Of all Tombstone's business, the restaurant business remained in operation with little trouble. The Can Can, one of Tombstone's favorite restaurants, continued to serve meals, and, unusually, its proprietor had not changed until now. Andrew Walsh, who had owned the Can Can since 1881, leased the business to John Watson. Prior to running the Can Can, Watson had been a machinist in Tombstone, and before that, had been a miner in Bisbee. Watson, in keeping with the times, changed the restaurant's fare. The Can Can now offered the choicest steaks, roast pig stuffed, chops, cutlets, and custard pie. Also available, was spring chicken and fresh eggs from its own poultry yards. Watson displayed his bountiful fare in the show windows of his restaurant for all to see.

Mother Nature was not too kind to Tombstone in 1887. On top of the mines flooding, an earthquake shook Tombstone's residents and buildings in early May. Mr. Storm and Mr. Abbott gave one report of the quake. They reported that a rush of water flooded the Sulphur Spring valley. They also reported that about one and one-half miles from Abbott's house water shot out of the ground reaching a height of about four to five feet and extending to about 100 feet in distance. Other than a few cracked walls, Tombstone was barely affected by the sudden quake.

The ladies of the Methodist Church certainly did not let a little thing like an earthquake get in the way of their fund-raising activities, and on May 5 they held a strawberry and ice cream festival to raise funds for the parsonage. They sold ice cream, strawberries and cake. It was reported that the fund-raiser was a "grand success, both socially and financially."

Lack of funds caused a local meat merchant to be involved in a legal proceeding. Apollinar Bauer and C. L. Cummings of the Tombstone Wholesale Butcher Company filed a complaint against Charles Bacigalupi for not paying them $136.10 for meat he purchased. Since he had not yet satisfied his debt, he was required to appear before Judge William Shearer to respond to the complaint on June 8. Just how he satisfied the debt is uncertain, but in April of the following year, Charles and his wife deeded their butcher shop and residence to Apollinar Bauer. They may have served as collateral until the Bacigalupi's could raise the money to cover the outstanding debt. If so, Bacigalupi must have satisfied this debt because in June 1888, Bauer deeded the property, known as Charley's Meat Market, back to Bacigalupi and his wife.

. To satisfy their customers, the town's grocery merchants made changes to enhance their city. The first was at the request of a female patron. A woman requested that when grocers set their vegetables outside for display, that they place them on taller boxes or boxes that were completely covered. She was slightly concerned that the vegetables were only covered with wire screens, and were at the "dog watering mark." The other change was also for the ladies, but at the request of the merchants. To accommodate their female patrons, the merchants requested that empty beer barrels be removed from the sidewalks so the women could visit their stores.

Even in its decline, Tombstone managed to find ways to celebrate, which probably helped the residents maintain a hopeful attitude. On one evening, the residents enjoyed a comic vocalist's performance at the Bird Cage Theatre. Most businesses were managing to get by, and life in Tombstone went on as usual. By fall, Tombstone was ready to celebrate Thanksgiving again. It always seemed to be a very celebrated holiday in Tombstone, or at least one that received a lot of attention. Like the previous Thanksgivings in Tombstone, people went to private parties, had quiet family gatherings, or dined out. The *Maison Doree* continued the tradition of serving the usual turkey dinner with all the trimmings, along with fish, regular dinner entrees, vegetables, and desserts served in the French style. The year of 1887 ended with the strong hope that Tombstone would somehow "get back to normal." That hope was thwarted by an underlying fear that it would not.

The year 1888 started uneventfully and more or less ended that way. Most businesses in town continued. Few changes took place. Tombstone's hotel accommodations totaled six: the Occidental, the Russ House, the Grand Central Lodging House, the Palace Lodging House, the American Lodging House, and the Railroad Hotel.

The restaurants now totaled eight and included the Can Can, the Elite, the Russ House, the Occidental, Gregory's, the New York Restaurant, the *Maison Doree*, and W.A. Anderson's Pacific Chop House. The Pacific Chop House continued to prepare meals for the city's prisoners as it had in the past.

The town also had two bakeries; one was owned by W.D. Coleman, former owner of the Pacific Chop House, and the other by R.A. Woodbury. Frank Yaple's confectionery and ice cream store continued to serve tempting treats. The butchers, who had approximately numbered eleven in number in 1883, now totaled four.

Tombstone had been accustomed to a variety of large mercantile firms, but now there were mostly small shops. These merchants were J.B. Angius, Samuel Barrow, Fitts Brothers, Mrs. Louden, G. Nardini, N. Nobile, John Prindiville and Charles Tarbell, who was also the undertaker. The three larger grocery merchants still in town were Sydow & Kieke, Meyer Brothers, and Frank Wolcott. Wolcott was still importing oysters to Tombstone by first-class mail, and could not keep them in stock due to their popularity.

The residents of Tombstone who remained occupied themselves with trying to make a living, attending church, gambling, and participating in social events and parties. It was hard for these pioneers to eventually admit that they would eventually have to give up their dream and move on. One such party took place in early 1889 was held at the Masonic Hall. A camp fire was held indoors, and the tables were filled with chicken, an abundance of beans, sandwiches, wine, beer, claret, and coffee. Other tables held a large box of tobacco with an assortment of clay pipes for the men to enjoy after their meal.

In the year 1889, more and more people were forced to realize that the bustling Tombstone of several years ago was forever gone. This happened despite the latest mining reports that indicated a new find in the Tombstone district. This find did put miners back to work, but only temporarily. One of those people was Otto Geisenhofer, who spent ten years of his life in Tombstone. Geisenhofer left Tombstone the following year and he purchased the Waldorf Hotel in Bisbee. He also ran his own butcher shop there. He eventually married a French woman and moved again to San Leandro, California, with his new bride. He stated that, "Arizona was no place for a lady."

Geisenhofer was not the only pioneer to leave Tombstone. Many other pioneers were leaving to investigate the prospects of a new mining camp in the Centennial district, near Yuma. Joseph Pascholy, who had been in the hotel business for years, was one of them. Nellie Cashman was also at the new mining camp, where she was about to establish a restaurant. Some remarked that it was like an early Tombstone reunion. She and Pascholy met many of Tombstone's pioneers, including Wyatt Earp. Earp, who had arrived with confectioner Frank Yaple and merchant Emil Sydow, also visited the new camp, but had returned to Tombstone promptly. The possibility of another "Tombstone" was quickly dissolved. Pascholy left, and opened the Huachuca Hotel in Ft. Huachuca a year later. He also suffered a personal tragedy, when his infant son suddenly passed away. Nellie Cashman had moved on to Prescott, to open yet another restaurant.

Tombstone once again fell victim to Mother Nature's wrath. Another cyclone was first sighted coming from the south pass of the Dragoon mountains some ten miles away. The cyclone's center approached Sixth and Allen Streets and leveled a vacant carpenter building. Awnings were ripped from their buildings, signs were blown away and roofs were torn from their respective houses. Merchant Frank Moore's cottonwood trees, the last ones in Tombstone, were destroyed when the cyclone uprooted and leveled them. The Tribolets' corral, located below town, did not escape the cyclone's path. It was leveled, and the newly purchased one-hundred head of steer were freed to roam Cochise County.

Sigfried Tribolet remained a butcher in town, and carried a wide variety of meats, including ham, bacon, eastern pickled pork, corned beef, and pig's feet. Along with their Tombstone meat market, they had one in Bisbee. The Tribolets also owned the lot where the Can Can was located on Allen Street. The restaurant was still going strong, but it was about to be moved to the corner of 4th & Allen Streets. Armand and Amelia Tuquet, opened the *Maison Doree* at the Can Can's old location, where their one-year lease with the property's owner, Sigfried Tribolet, cost $60 per month. Once the Can Can was re-opened at 4th & Allen Streets in 1890, Nellie Walsh, and Andrew Walsh, became the proprietors. The Can Can continued to serve oysters and fresh fish every day. Andrew Walsh also had another Can Can restaurant in Bisbee, but was preparing to sell it. The Walsh's remained the proprietors for at least another year, and the next owners were Mr. & Mrs. John Henninger, who had come to town in 1886. The Can Can was of the few restaurants that had stayed in continuous operation since its early beginning, but it too eventually closed after the turn of the century.

Mining, the driving force behind Tombstone, continued on a very small scale, but the milling of the ore was moved. Ore was now being shipped out of town to various places for processing because it was more cost effective. This limited mining allowed Tombstone to remain in existence.

Tombstone's residents refused to give up the dream of being the most prosperous town in Arizona. In an effort to remain prosperous, they tried to lure people to town for reasons other than mining. They claimed, and rightly so, that Tombstone was a well-planned town with broad streets. They boasted their climate was healthful with warm summer days and cool, pleasant nights. Their water was clear, sparkling, and sweet. In spite of their efforts, people continued to leave Tombstone for something better, and its population steadily declined. Even though Tombstone's future was uncertain for many years, one thing its residents could count on was its first-class accommodations and fine dining establishments. Though there are a number of ways that one can obtain a sense of the rise and fall of this once great mining town, the history of its food industry is one of the most interesting.

CHAPTER SEVEN

BILLS OF FARE & RECIPES

BAKERY, ICE CREAM PARLOR, AND CONFECTIONERY RECIPES

OTTO GEISENHOFER'S ZIMSTERNE C. 1880
(Cinnamon Stars—a traditional German Christmas cookie)

Otto, like many cooks of the time, was not always exact in measuring for his recipes. My Grandmother and my husband's Grandmother were the same way. If you asked them how much of an ingredient to use, they would reply, "oh, a handful, or the size of an egg." Otto's recipes are uniquely written, which is why I have provided you with his exact recipe, along with one I modified for you to use.

4 eggs whites, beaten solid (called "snow" in German)	1/4 c. candied lemon peel
	1/4 c. candied orange peel
2 tsp. cinnamon, minced	1/4 tsp. baking soda
1 1/2 c. sugar	1 c. flour for rolling
1/2 c. unpeeled almonds, ground	

In a large bowl beat the egg whites until soft peaks form. Gradually add the cinnamon and sugar and continue beating until the egg whites are shining, about 10 minutes. Gently fold in the almonds, candied peel, and baking soda. Add enough of the flour to allow you to roll out the dough 1/4" thick. Cut with a star cookie cutter and place on a cookie sheet lined with paper. Allow the cookies to rest overnight. The next day, bake them at 325° for 15 minutes.

Here is the translated recipe, as Otto wrote it. I reduced the quantity and added some instructions:

7 egg whites, beaten solid   1/4 lb. citronat
1 lb. sugar   1/4 lb. orangeat
1 lb. unpeeled almonds
Cinnamon, minced, soda, some flour and let stand overnight.

OTTO GEISENHOFER'S ZIMNTWAFFALER
C. 1880
(Cinnamonwaffles)

These are traditionally eaten as snacks in Germany, but they also make an extra special breakfast treat.

1 3/4 c. sugar	2 tsp. cinnamon
3 eggs	4 c. flour
2 sticks butter	

Beat the sugar and eggs in a large mixing bowl until thick and foamy, about 10 minutes. While this is mixing, melt the butter in a pan over medium heat. Slowly add the melted butter to the beaten egg mass. Mix well, but be sure to leave a little melted butter on the bottom of the bowl. To check this, stop mixing and drag the beaters through the mixture. You should be able to see the separation.

Next, add the cinnamon and as much of the flour to form 1-inch balls of dough. Place the balls on a hot waffle iron and cook until light brown (about 2 minutes). Allow these to cool if you are eating them the traditional German way. If you are having them for breakfast, serve warm with butter and syrup. Makes about 30 2-inch waffles.

Here is the translated recipe, as Otto wrote it. I reduced the quantity and added some instructions:

1 lb. sugar	*1-2 coffeespoons cinnamon*
6 eggs	*about 1/2 flour*
3/4-1 lb. butter	

Sugar and eggs are beaten until thick and foamy. Meanwhile melt butter. Add butter slowly to beaten mass, but so that something stays at the bottom of the bowl. Add cinnamon and as much flour as needed to form small balls. These are baked in a hot waffle iron until light brown.

OTTO GEISENHOFER'S BUTTERGEBACKENES ZUM AUSTECHEN C. 1880
(Butter cookies for cutting)

2 c. butter	4 c. flour
2/3 c. sugar	1 tsp. baking soda
3 egg yolks	peel of 1 lemon, diced finely
1/2 c. grated almonds	

Beat butter, sugar and egg yolks for 20 minutes (this will give the batter volume); set aside. Add the remaining ingredients and blend well. Roll dough out to 1/2" thickness and cut out cookies and let stand over night. Bake on an ungreased cookie sheet at 300° for 15 minutes. Good for Anise cookies. Makes 6 dozen 2" round cookies.

Here is the translated recipe, as Otto wrote it. I reduced the quantity and added some instructions:

1 lb. butter	*1/2 lb. grated almonds*
3/4 lb. sugar	*1 lb. flour*
5 egg yolks	*2 knife points baking soda*
beat for 1 hour to 1 side	*peel of 2 lemons*

Cut out cookies and let stand overnight. Bake at 300 degrees. Good for Anise cookies.

Good For 1 Loaf of Bread   *M. Geisenhofer*

OTTO GEISENHOFER'S GUILE WEISSE NURNBERGER LEBKUCKEN C. 1880
(Good White Nurnberger Cookies)

1 1/3 c. sugar	1/4 c. slivered almonds
4 whole eggs	1 tsp. cinnamon
peel of 1 lemon, diced	1/4 tsp. ground clove
1/4 c. candied lemon peel	1/2 tsp. soda
1/4 c. candied orange peel	2 c. flour
juice of 1/2 lemon	

Beat the sugar and eggs for 30 minutes until very thick and foamy. Add the remaining ingredients in the order that they are given, and mix well.

Put as much dough as you can handle on a floured board, roll it out and cut into shapes. Grease the cookie sheets with butter, put pieces on there, not too close together, and bake at 350° for 10 minutes. Do not allow to brown. Makes 4 dozen 3-inch cookies.

Here is the translated recipe, as Otto wrote it. I reduced the quantity and added some instructions:

Beat 500 gr. (1 lb.) very fine sugar and 4 whole eggs for 1/2 hour until foamy, add the peel of lemon, 1 handful zitronat (depending on one's taste), 1 handful orangeat (depending on one's taste), both cut into small pieces, juice of half a lemon, fine pieced almonds, 1 tsp. cinnamon, 1 knifepoint stomped clove, 1/2 tsp. soda, and at last 1 lb. flour. Put dough on a board and roll it out into pieces (whatever pieces you want). Cover baking sheet with butter, put pieces on there, not to close together, and bake at moderate heat (350 degrees).

OTTO GEISENHOFER'S SPRINGERELE C. 1880

1 1/3 c. sugar	2 1/2 c. flour
2 eggs	1/2 tsp. baking powder
1 T. anise	peel of 1 lemon, finely chopped

Beat the sugar and eggs in a large mixing bowl for 30 minutes. Next, add flour, anise, lemon peel, and baking powder. Mix well and then turn the dough out on to a heavily floured board to incorporate completely. Only knead the dough enough the make it the right consistency for rolling.

Roll the dough out until 1/2-inch thick. Press the floured wooden forms or rolling pin on the dough so that imprint is seen clearly on dough. Remove forms carefully. Use a dough cutter or knife and cut out the pieces. Add some fresh dough to the rest before rolling out again. Butter the baking sheet and sprinkle it with some flour and anise seeds. The cookies must now rest overnight before baking. The next day bake them in a 350° oven. Do not allow them to brown. Makes about 2 dozen.

Here is the translated recipe, as Otto wrote it. I reduced the quantity and added some instructions:

1 lb. sugar	1 lb. flour
4 eggs	peel from 1 lemon
1 handful anise	butter for baking sheet

Sugar and eggs are beaten for 3/4 to 1 hour, then add flour, anise, and lemon peel, and also 1 teaspoon baking powder if you please, and then process dough on a board thoroughly. It is good if one leaves some flour for processing the dough. Then roll weakly until finger thick good rubbed with flour, press the floured wooden forms on the dough so that imprint is seen clearly on dough. Remove forms carefully, now use a dough cutter or knife and cut out the pieces. Add some fresh dough to the rest before rolling out again. The baking sheet is covered with thin butter layer, if you please, covered with some flour and anise, the dough pieces placed on it and placed overnight in not so warm room to dry. The next day they are baked in a medium hot oven, so that they stay light and get small feet. Oven 350 degrees.

HOT ROLLS.

1 T. dry yeast	2 T. melted butter
1 1/2 c. water (110°)	or margarine
2 tsp. salt	4 1/2-5 c. bread flour
corn meal	

Dissolve the yeast in a 1/2 cup of the warm water, in a large bowl. In a separate bowl, combine the salt and the rest of the warm water. Pour this into the yeast mixture. Add in 4 cups of the flour and mix well. If the dough seems sticky, gradually add additional flour as needed. Turn out onto a floured surface and knead for 10 minutes, or until a springy and smooth dough is achieved. Place the dough in a lightly oiled bowl, cover and allow to rise until doubled in a warm place (75°-80°). This should take about 2 hours. Punch the dough down and allow it to rise for another hour. Punch down again and tear off pieces the size of a medium onion. Cup your hands and roll the dough into a ball. Place 2" apart on a cookie sheet that has been sprinkled with corn meal. Continuing doing this until all the dough has been used. Using the palm of your hand, flatten each roll. Cover and allow to rise until double, about 45 minutes. Brush the loaves with the melted butter and bake at 425° for 15 minutes.

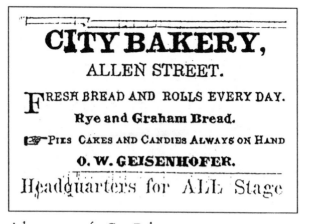

CITY BAKERY,

ALLEN STREET.

FRESH BREAD AND ROLLS EVERY DAY.

Rye and Graham Bread.

☞ PIES CAKES AND CANDIES ALWAYS ON HAND

O. W. GEISENHOFER.

Headquarters for ALL Stage

Advertisement for City Bakery   Tombstone Epitaph, 1880

WHITE BREAD.

1 pkg. yeast	1 tsp. salt
1 T. sugar	2 eggs, lightly beaten
1/4 c. warm water—110°	3-3 1/2 c. bread flour
1/4 c. butter, softened	2 tsp. butter, melted
1/4 c. milk, scalded—110°	

In a small bowl, combine the yeast and sugar. Pour the warm water over this and set aside. Now put the scalded milk, butter, and salt in a large mixing bowl. Add the yeast mixture, eggs, and 1 cup of the flour. Mix well, and add enough additional flour to form a soft, but not sticky dough. Knead on a floured surface for about 10 minutes. You will know that you have kneaded enough when you press a finger in the dough and it bounces back. Place the dough in a lightly oiled bowl, turn to coat the surface, and cover with a towel or plastic wrap. Allow the dough to double in size; this should take about an hour, and be done in a warm place.

Remove the dough from the bowl and roll into a rectangular shape, on a floured surface. Starting at the shortest end, roll up like a jelly roll. Tuck the ends under and place in a greased 9-inch loaf pan. Allow this to rise until double under a towel, in a warm place. Once the dough has risen again, brush the top with the melted butter and bake at 375° for 30 minutes. Remove the bread from the pan and cool on a cake rack.

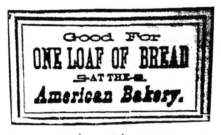

American Bakery Ticket, 1881

Silver Lady Antiques

FRENCH BREAD.

1 pkg. yeast	1 tsp. salt
1 1/4 c. water (110°)	cornmeal
1 lb., 2 oz. bread flour	

Dissolve the yeast in the water in a large bowl. Let stand for 5 minutes, then stir. Mix the salt in with the flour. Add 4 cups of the flour to the yeast mixture and mix for 10 minutes. The dough should be soft, but not sticky. Turn out onto a floured surface and knead in the remaining flour until you have a firm and springy dough. This should take about 15 minutes. To test, press a finger in the dough; if it bounces back, it's done. This can also be kneaded with a good mixer, for about 5 minutes.

Place the dough in a lightly oiled bowl, cover and allow to rise in a warm (70°-75°) place, until doubled; about 2 hours. Punch the dough down, recover, and let rise for an additional hour and a half. Punch down one last time, and divide in half. Turn the dough out onto a lightly floured surface and roll into a rectangular shape. From the long side, fold the dough a third of the way towards the center and press down seam. Fold the other long side in the same fashion. Using the palms of your hands, roll the dough back and forth to form a long roll. Place on a baking sheet that has been sprinkled with cornmeal. Cover and let rise in a warm place until doubled, about 1 1/2 hours. Place a pan of boiling water in the bottom of the oven and bake the loaves at 450° for 30-40 minutes. When done, the bread will sound hollow when tapped. Remove the bread from the baking sheet and allow to cool, by standing them upright to let the air circulate around them.

SOURDOUGH BREAD.

1 c. sourdough starter 1 T. sugar
1/2 c. milk, lukewarm 2 1/2-3 c. bread flour
1 tsp. salt

Place starter in a large bowl; add the milk and stir. Next add the salt and sugar; stir again. Add the flour and mix until well combined. Knead the dough on a lightly floured surface for about 10 minutes. Put the dough in a lightly oiled bowl and cover. Let the dough rise in a warm (75°-80°) place until doubled, about an hour. Punch down and let rise a second time. Punch down again, shape the dough, and place in a greased loaf pan. Cover the dough and allow it to rise until doubled. Bake at 400° for 40-45 minutes. Remove from the pan and let cool on a cake rack.

SOURDOUGH STARTER

2 c. potato water 1 T. sugar
2 c. flour

Combine the above in a glass bowl and allow to stand, covered, in a warm place for 48-72 hours to ferment. Once it has begun to ferment, and smells sour, it's ready. It should look like pancake batter. Store in the refrigerator (not too cold— around 45°), covered until ready to use. When you're ready to use the starter, remove the amount you need, and allow it to come to room temperature. Once you remove some of the starter, you will need to replenish it. For example, of you remove 1 cup of starter, add 1 cup of flour, 1 cup of water and 1 tablespoon of sugar back in. Stir to combine and store in the refrigerator.

PREMIUM CHOCOLATE.

This yummy hot chocolate was served at many of Tombstone's bakeries and coffee shops.

1 c. hot milk	1 sq. chocolate, sweetened
1 c. boiling water	1 T. sugar

Bring the water to a boil over high heat, in a medium sauce pan. Add the milk and heat through. Next add the chocolate and sugar and boil for 5 minutes. Serve in coffee mugs or tea cups with a dollop of whipped cream. Makes 2 cups.

STRAWBERRY ICE CREAM.

2 c. sugar	1 qt. heavy cream
1 pt. milk	2 c. strawberries, pureed
1 tsp. cornstarch	1 tsp. vanilla
1 egg, beaten well	

Heat sugar, milk, cornstarch and egg in a large saucepan over medium low heat. Stir to combine, and cook until cornstarch has dissolved; let cool. Once cooled, add the cream, vanilla and strawberry puree. Freeze according to ice cream machine instructions. Makes 4 quarts.

ICE-CREAM SALOON,

BANNING & SHAW

Have always on hand the best ice-cream and fresh home made candies. Ladies and gentlemen please give us a call.

Fourth Street, Above Fremont.

Daily Nugget, 1881

STRAWBERRY SHORTCAKE.

Strawberry shortcake is always a dessert success, as the ladies of the Methodist church could have attested to.

5 1/2 c. strawberries	1/2 tsp. salt
1/4 c. sugar	1/2 c. butter
2 c. flour	1 egg, beaten
3 T. sugar	2/3 c. milk
1 T. baking powder	whipped cream filling*

Place the strawberries in a bowl and sprinkle with 1/4 cup sugar; set aside. Meanwhile, put the dry ingredients in a large bowl and mix with a whisk. Add the butter and cut in with a pastry cutter until crumbly. In a small bowl, mix the egg and the milk together. Pour over the crumbled mixture and stir just enough to moisten.

Spread this into a greased 8" cake pan, and bake at 450° for 15 minutes. Allow the cake to cool in the pan for 10 minutes, then remove. When cool enough to handle, horizontally cut the cake in half. Spread a layer of the whipped cream on the cake, and them a layer of the strawberries. Put the top on the cake and frost with the whipped cream and strawberries. Serve warm.

*See recipe on page 196.

CANDIED ORANGE PEEL.

This confection was very popular, not just for eating, but for baking as well. The recipe is a little time-consuming, so you may want to do it on a rainy day, or over the weekend. It also makes for a special treat around the holidays.

5 large oranges	2 c. sugar
Juice of 5 oranges	1/2 c. sugar for dipping

Peel the oranges with a potato peeler, being sure not to remove the pith or white part, which is bitter. Slice the orange peels into strips. Squeeze the juice from the oranges and set aside. Bring the pot of water to a boil and place orange peel into it. Be sure to change the water twice before the oranges become tender. To do this, drain the oranges and replenish with boiling water that you have waiting in a tea kettle.

While this is boiling, squeeze the juice of the oranges into a bowl. In a medium saucepan, combine the sugar and orange juice. Once the orange peels are tender—about 20 minutes, place into the orange juice and sugar. Allow to boil for 20 minutes over medium heat. Strain and place peels on wax paper. Using a fork, spread the peels apart and allow to cool. When the peels are cool enough to handle, dip them in sugar and allow to harden overnight. If you will be using the orange peels in a cake or cookie recipe, omit the sugar dipping step.

Note: Lemons can be substituted for this recipe, but you will need to add an additional cup of sugar

CHOCOLATE CARAMELS.

1 1/4 c. sugar
1/2 c. corn syrup
1/4 c. butter
pinch of cream of tartar

1 1/2 c. milk
1 1/2 sq. unsweetened
   baking chocolate
1/2 tsp. vanilla

Combine the first 4 ingredients and 3/4 cup of the milk in a large heavy bottomed saucepan. Bring the mixture to a boil and cook for 7 minutes. Gradually add the remaining milk and continue boiling until the mixture thickens (246° on a candy thermometer). Add the chocolate and vanilla and turn into a buttered pan. While the candy is still warm, cut into squares. Allow to cool and enjoy.

CHOCOLATE CREAM DROPS.

2 c. sugar
1/3 c. water
1 tsp. butter
2/3 c. milk

1 tsp. vanilla
3 sq. sweetened chocolate,
   melted

Boil sugar, milk, butter and water for 20 minutes in a heavy duty saucepan. Add vanilla and remove from heat, stir constantly until cool enough to handle. Place chocolate in a double boiler and melt; set aside. Form the candy into 1/2" balls. Once the candy had cooled, roll it in the melted chocolate. Allow to cool and harden on waxed paper.

VANILLA ICE CREAM.

1 qt. heavy cream
1 pt. milk
2 c. sugar

1 egg, beaten well
1 tsp. vanilla
1 tsp. cornstarch

Heat sugar, milk, cornstarch and egg in a large saucepan over medium low heat. Stir to combine and cook until cornstarch has dissolved; let cool. Once cooled, add the cream and vanilla. Freeze according to ice cream machine instructions. Makes 4 quarts.

CHOCOLATE ICE CREAM.

2 c. sugar
1 pt. milk
1 tsp. cornstarch
1 egg, beaten well

8 oz. dark chocolate
1 tsp. vanilla
1 qt. heavy cream

Heat sugar, milk, cornstarch, egg and chocolate in a large saucepan over medium low heat. Stir to combine, and cook until the chocolate has melted; let cool. Once cooled, add the cream and vanilla. Freeze according to ice cream machine instructions. Makes 4 quarts.

FRANK YAPLE,
Manufacturing Confectoner

76 Fifth Street, Tombstone, Arizona.

THE FINEST LINE OF CANDIES IN THE TERRITORY.

ICE CREAM AND TOYS IN THIER SEASON.

McKenney's 1882 Business Directory

GROCERY STORE RECIPES

CHOW CHOW.

1 large cauliflower	1 gallon white vinegar
12 small cucumbers	6 T. ground mustard
2 bunches celery	1 tsp. freshly ground pepper
1 doz. small onions	1 tsp. whole cloves
3 red peppers	1 cinnamon stick
2 c. green beans	2 tsp. turmeric
4 carrots, cut into strips	1/4 c. salt

Cut all the vegetables, except carrots, into small pieces and place in a large bowl. Sprinkle with salt and let stand for 24 hours. Drain off any excess liquid. In a large stockpot, bring the vinegar and spices to a boil. Add the vegetables and continue cooking until slightly tender. Pack into hot pint jars, being sure to leave 1/2" headspace in the jars. Tighten the lids and set in boiling water that covers the jars. When the water begins to boil again, cook for 15 minutes. Remove from the water and set on counter to cool. Yields about 6 pints.

Advertisement for Fitzhenry & Mansfield
Tombstone Epitaph, 1884

PICALLILI.

4 c. green tomatoes, diced	1/2 c. horseradish
4 green peppers, diced	1 tsp. mustard seed, ground
2 onions, diced	1/2 oz. whole cloves
1 small head cabbage, diced	1 tsp. ground cinnamon
1 c. celery, chopped	1 c. salt
3 c. vinegar	

Place the chopped vegetables in a large stock pot and sprinkle with salt, let stand overnight. Drain off any liquid; add the vinegar and remaining ingredients. Cook until slightly tender; stirring occasionally.

Fill pint jars, leaving a 1/2" head space and seal. Place the pints in boiling water. When the water returns to the boil, cook for 15 minutes. Remove and allow to cool. Makes 12 pints.

BAKING POWDER BISCUITS.

4 c. flour	1 tsp. salt
3 tsp. baking powder	1 c. water
4 T. shortening	1/2 c. milk

ROYAL
BAKING
POWDER
Absolutely Pure.

This powder never varies. A marvel of purity, strength and wholesomeness. More economical than the ordinary kinds, and cannot be sold in competition with the multitude of low test, short weight, alum or phosphate powders. Sold only in cans. ROYAL BAKING POWDER Co., 106 Wall street, N Y

Tombstone Epitaph, 1882

Mix the dry ingredients together in a large bowl. Cut the shortening into the flour with a pastry blender or two knives. Add the water and stir just to mix, do not over beat the batter or the biscuits will become tough. If the dough looks too dry add more water. Roll the dough to a 1/4" thickness on heavily floured surface. Cut the biscuits with a biscuit cutter and place on a greased baking sheet. Bake at 425° for 10 minutes, or until done.

Note: For an extra special treat, try adding 1/2 cup of shredded cheese and a half teaspoon of your favorite herb to the batter before rolling.

MOLASSES COOKIES.
(My Great Grandmother Osgood's)

I remember going to visit my Great Grandmother Osgood at her farmhouse in Pennsylvania when I was a little girl. As soon as I walked in the door (after I had pet all the cats and kittens on my way in), there were two or three cookie jars filled with giant molasses and sugar cookies. Just thinking about it brings back wonderful memories.

4 c. flour, sifted	1/2 c. shortening
4 tsp. baking soda	1 c. sugar
4 tsp. cinnamon	1 egg
1 tsp. cloves	1 c. molasses
2 tsp. salt	1 c. milk

Sift the flour, soda, spices and salt together in a small bowl; set aside. In a large bowl, cream the shortening and sugar. Next, add the egg and mix well; stir in the molasses and milk. Gradually the flour mixture to the molasses mixture until well blended.

Drop by teaspoonful onto a lightly greased cookie sheet. Bake at 425° for 8 minutes.

Yield—5 dozen.

Louisiana molasses at $1.25 per gallon also a fine assortment of Louisiana sugar just received at Joe Hoefler's.

Tombstone Epitaph, 1886

MEAT MARKET RECIPES

PORK SAUSAGE.

5 lb. Boston butt roast	1 T. parsley
2 c. onions, minced	3 T. sage
1/2 tsp. cayenne pepper	1 tsp. salt
1/4 tsp. freshly ground pepper	

Press the pork through the meat grinder to grind finely. Place in a bowl, and add the remaining ingredients and mix well. Press this through the meat grinder again to ensure the sausage is well seasoned. If you want to check for seasonings, do not eat the raw meat. Take a little piece of the sausage and fry it, then taste it, and adjust the seasoning if needed. Shape into patties or stuff into sausage casings.

ITALIAN SAUSAGE.

2 lb. Boston butt roast	1 1/2 T. parsley, dried
1 T. fennel seed	3 garlic cloves, crushed
1 bay leaf, crushed	1 tsp. red pepper flakes
1 tsp. salt	4 T. white wine
1/4 tsp. freshly ground pepper	

Press the pork through the meat grinder to grind finely. Place in a bowl, and add the remaining ingredients and mix well. Press this through the meat grinder again to ensure the sausage is well seasoned. If you want to check for seasonings, do not eat the raw meat. Take a little piece of the sausage and fry it, then taste it, and adjust the seasoning if needed. Shape into patties or stuff into sausage casings.

RESTAURANT RECIPES

BAKED BEANS.

4 c. pea beans	3 T. brown sugar
1/2 lb. salt pork or bacon	1 c. boiling water
1 tsp. baking soda	1 c. tomato sauce
1 T. salt	1/2 tsp. mustard
2 T. molasses	

Cover the beans with water and allow to soak overnight. Drain the beans and add enough water to cover them again, along with the baking soda. Simmer until the bean skins burst; about 30 minutes. Drain and place in a deep baking dish.

Score the rind of the salt pork and place in the dish with the beans. Be sure to leave the rind exposed when placing it in the beans. If using bacon, cut into 1/4 inch pieces.

Combine the salt, molasses, sugar, mustard and tomato sauce in a bowl, blend well. Add the boiling water to this, stir well and pour over the beans. Make sure to add enough boiling water to cover the beans completely. Place a cover or aluminum foil over beans and bake at 300° for 6-8 hours, or until beans are soft. Uncover the beans during the last hour of cooking.

Note: If the beans become dry, additional boiling water may be added up to the last hour of cooking.

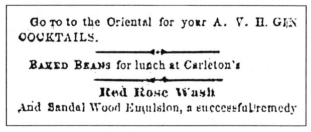

Tombstone Epitaph, 1880

BUTTERMILK HOT CAKES.

2 1/2 c. flour 1 T. sugar
1 tsp. salt 1 1/2 c. buttermilk
1/2 tsp. baking powder water

In a large bowl, sift dry ingredients. Add the milk and egg and enough water to get a good consistency. Using a ladle or spoon, pour batter onto a hot greased griddle or frying pan. Cook over medium high heat until bubbles appear on the batter. Turn and cook for about a minute longer. Serve warm with butter and maple syrup. Garnish with orange slices or wedges.

Note: If you do not have buttermilk, add 1 tsp. vinegar to 1 cup of milk. Let stand for 5 minutes, then stir and use.

Rural House Bill of Fare   *Tombstone Epitaph, 1880*

Grand Hotel Bill of Fare　　　　　*Tombstone Epitaph, 1881*

CHICKEN SOUP.

3-4 lb. chicken, quartered　　1 c. milk
1 c. celery, chopped　　　　　1 T. parsley, chopped
1 onion, chopped　　　　　　1/2 tsp. salt
2-3 qts. water　　　　　　　1/4 tsp. freshly ground pepper
1 T. butter　　　　　　　　1 T. flour

Place chicken, celery, onion and water in a large stock pot. Boil for about 45 minutes or until the chicken is tender. Skim off the top of the stock, remove and de-bone the chicken. Strain and measure 5 cups of the stock; set aside. In the same stock pot, melt the butter and add the flour to make a *roux*. Cook over medium heat for about 3 minutes. Whisking constantly, slowly stir in the chicken stock. Add the remaining ingredients and simmer for 5 minutes.

SALMON, HOLLANDAISE SAUCE.

1/2 tsp. salt	2 lb. salmon, cut into
1 slice of onion	serving pieces
1/2 tsp. peppercorns	1 c. water
1 slice of lemon	1 c. white wine
1 bay leaf	

Place all the ingredients in a large skillet and bring to a simmer. Cover and continue cooking for about 10 minutes. The fish is done when a fork pierces it easily. Remove from the pan and place on a serving platter. Pour Hollandaise sauce over the pieces. Garnish with dill weed.

HOLLANDAISE SAUCE

1/2 c. butter, cut into pieces	1/4 tsp. salt
2 tsp. vinegar	pinch cayenne pepper
2 egg yolks, beaten	

In a medium double boiler, place vinegar, eggs yolks and a third of the butter. Cook over boiling water; stirring constantly for 2 minutes. Add the second third of the butter and whisk to blend. Once the sauce begins to thicken, add the final third of the butter and whisk to incorporate. Remove from the heat and add the salt and cayenne pepper.

RIBS OF BEEF.

1 lb. beef ribs, uncut	1 bouquet garni*
salt & pepper to season	2 garlic cloves, minced
1/2 c. butter or margarine	1/2 tsp. salt & pepper
1 T. oil	2 c. fresh mushrooms, sliced
1 large onion, chopped	2 T. flour
4 oz. bacon, diced	2 c. warm water

Preheat oven to 350°. Melt half the butter and oil in a large dutch oven, over medium high heat. Sprinkle the ribs with salt and pepper, then brown the ribs on both sides. Place the onions and bacon around the ribs. Add the water, bouquet garni and garlic. Sprinkle with salt and pepper. Bring this to a boil. Place in the oven and cook for 2 hours or until meat is tender. Add the mushrooms and cook an additional hour. When done, put the ribs in a deep serving platter.

Combine the remaining the butter and flour in a small sauce pan to make a roux. Cook for about 2 minutes, or until smooth. Stirring constantly, add to boiling pot liquid to make a gravy. Pour over ribs and serve immediately.

*BOUQUET GARNI.

1 sprig thyme	10-12 parsley stems
1 bay leaf	

The herbs may be tied together or placed in a piece of cheesecloth and then tied together.

Note: Try grilling the ribs for a different flavor. To do this, cook the ribs on the grill just until both sides have been browned, then proceed with the recipe.

CHICKEN FRICASSEE.

3 lb. chicken, cut	1/2 tsp. tarragon
1 onion, quartered	2 c. dry white wine
4 T. flour	2 c. chicken stock
1/2 lb. mushrooms, quartered	1/2 c. heavy cream
1 tsp. oil	juice of 1/2 lemon
4 T. butter	

Melt the butter and oil in a large stock pot over medium heat. Sprinkle the chicken with salt and pepper; add to the pot. Cook the chicken until it is firm and lightly golden. Sprinkle the meat with the tarragon and add the onions. Cover the pot and cook for 10 more minutes. Uncover and sprinkle the chicken and onions with flour. Turn the chicken to coat evenly. Cook an additional 5 minutes. Gradually stir in the wine and stock; stir to combine. The chicken should be almost covered, if not, add more stock. Cover and simmer for 35 minutes. Add the mushrooms, and cream; simmer for an additional 10 minutes. Add the lemon juice. Check the seasoning, adjust if needed. Serve with rice.

BAKED OYSTER PIE.

4 c. medium oysters, fresh or canned	1 T. parsley, chopped
	2 1/2 c. chicken stock
3 medium potatoes, cubed	2 c. white sauce*
2 celery stalks, chopped	1 double pie crust recipe

Drain the oysters, reserving the liquor. Boil potatoes, celery, and parsley in the chicken stock for about 10 minutes or until tender. While this is cooking, make the white sauce. Place the oysters in the boiling potato water; allow to come back to the boil. Reduce heat and simmer until the edges of the oysters begin to curl. Remove from the heat; add the white sauce and stir. Allow this to cool. Line the bottom of an 8 x 12 baking dish with 1 pie crust. Fill with the oyster filling and cover with the second pie crust. Flute the edges and bake at 375° for 30 minutes or until golden.

*See recipe on page 132.

WHITE SAUCE.

4 T. butter
6 T. flour
2 c. milk

1/2 tsp. salt
1/4 tsp. freshly ground pepper

Melt the butter in a medium saucepan, over medium heat. When the butter begins to bubble; add the flour and seasonings. Stir and cook for 2 to 3 minutes to allow the flour to cook. Now, gradually add the milk and whisk constantly. Continue whisking until the sauce thickens. Makes 2 cups.

NEW POTATOES.

10-12 small new potatoes
1/4 c. butter
1 T. parsley

1/2 tsp. salt
1/4 tsp. freshly ground pepper

Peel and boil the potatoes in salted water for 15 minutes or until tender. Remove and drain. Melt the butter in a large skillet, over medium heat; add the potatoes. Sprinkle with the salt, pepper, and parsley. Cook long enough for the potatoes to be evenly coated with the seasonings.

ASPARAGUS.

1 lb. asparagus
1/2 tsp. salt

1 T. butter
1/4 tsp. freshly ground pepper

Wash the asparagus and cut off the ends. To know where to cut, hold the asparagus in your hands and bend them. The ends should snap off where the tender part ends and the tough part begins. Place the spears in a large pot of boiling, salted water. Cook for 15 minutes or until tender. Drain and toss with butter and salt and pepper.

GOOSEBERRY PIE.

4 c. fresh gooseberries
2/3 c. sugar
1/4 c. flour
1/8 tsp. salt

1 T. butter
recipe for 1 double pie crust,
   unbaked

Snip off the ends of the gooseberries and wash in water. Place the berries in a large bowl; add the sugar, flour and salt. Mix well.

Line a 9-inch pie and fill with the berries; dot the top with the butter and cover with second pie crust. Make 4 or 5 slits on the crust to allow the steam to escape. Bake at 375° for 45 minutes. If the crust starts to brown, cover it with aluminum foil. Cool before cutting.

QUEEN CHARLOTTE PUDDING.

2 c. fine bread crumbs
2 c. milk
1 c. sugar
4 egg yolks, beaten

grating of 1 lemon rind
juice of 1 lemon
4 egg whites
1/2 c. sugar

In a large bowl, combine the bread crumbs, milk, sugar, egg yolks, and lemon rind; stir well. Pour mixture into a deep baking dish and bake at 350° for 45-50 minutes, or until no longer watery.

In a separate bowl, beat the egg whites until stiff, gradually add the sugar and lemon juice to the whites. Spread a layer of your favorite jelly over the baked pudding, then pour the egg whites over the jelly. Bake in the oven just until the top browns lightly.

Allow to cool slightly before placing in the refrigerator and chill for at least 4 hours.

CITY ITEMS

RUSS HOUSE.

Sunday Dinner—Bill of Fare.

SOUPS.

Chicken,   Consomme.

FISH.

Lobster. Salad a la Mayonnaise,
Salmon, Egg Sauce.

BOILED.

Ham, Sauce au Champagne,
Tongue, Sauce Piquante,
Mutton. Caper Sauce,
Corned Beef.

ENTREES.

Chicken Saûte, a la Marengo,
Cotelettes d'Agneau, aux Champignons,
Chicken Giblets, a l'Parisienne,
Veal Fricandeau au Meadere,
Queen Fritters a la Victoria,
Macaroni a la Italienne,
Beuf a la Mode,
Veal Fricassee.

ROASTS.

Chicken, Short Ribs of Beef, Mutton,
Prime Beef, Lamb, Veal,
Pork and Apple Sauce.

VEGETABLES,

Green   Corn, Sugar Peas, Tomatoes,
String Beans and Potatoes.

PASTRY.

Blackberry, Peach and Custard Pies,
Assorted Cakes.

PUDDINGS.

Cocoanut, Cream Sauce,
Plum, Brandy Sauce.

DESERT.

Peaches, Plums and Grapes.

RELISHES.

Assorted.   Wines to order.

Russ House Bill of Fare   *Daily Nugget, 1881*

CONSOMMÉ.

3 lbs. lean round steak	1/4 c. shortening
1 lb. beef bones or beef ribs	2 T. salt
3 lbs. veal bones	1 tsp. whole peppercorns
1 qt. chicken stock	4 cloves
1 c. carrot, diced	3 sprigs of thyme
1 c. turnip, diced	1 sprig marjoram
1 c. celery, diced	2 sprigs parsley
1 onion, sliced	1 bay leaf
3 leeks, diced	7 qts. water
4 egg whites	

Cut beef into 1" cubes. Brown half the beef in the shortening in a large stock pot. Add the remaining meat, bones, and the water. Let stand for half an hour. Heat slowly to boiling, and simmer for 3 hours; remove scum as it forms.

Next, add the chicken stock and simmer for 1 additional hour. Add the vegetables and seasonings. Simmer for another hour. Remove any fat from the top, and strain the soup. Cool. Clarify the soup by adding the egg whites to the cooled consommé. Bring to a simmer over medium low heat, stirring constantly. Once the soup has reached a simmer, turn the heat up to medium. Allow the consommé to come to a slow boil, without stirring, and cook for 5 minutes. Remove from the heat and strain through a few layers of cheesecloth. Makes 5 1/2 qts.

BROWN STOCK.

4 lbs. cracked beef bones   4 whole garlic cloves
3 lbs. beef shank meat   6 parsley sprigs
2 carrots, peeled & quartered 1/4 tsp. thyme
2 onions, peeled & halved   1 bay leaf
1 1/2 c. water   2 tsp. salt
2 celery stalks, quartered

Place the bones, meat, carrots, and onions in an oven proof pan and cook for 35-40 minutes in a 450° oven. Turn occasionally to evenly brown. Once cooked, remove from the pan and set on a plate. Drain the oil from the roasting pan and discard. Add the water to the pan, and over high heat, scrape the bottom to remove browned bits. Once this is done add the remaining ingredients and enough cold water to cover all the ingredients in the pot. Add the salt and celery and stir.

Tie the garlic and herbs in cheesecloth and place in the pot. Allow this to simmer for 4 1/2 hours. Skim off any fat from the top. This stock can be used in a variety of recipes. Makes 4 qts.

CHICKEN SAUTÉ A LA MARENGO.

3-4 lb. chicken, cut into serving pieces	2 T. butter
	2 T. oil
1/2 tsp. salt	marengo sauce
1/8 tsp. freshly ground pepper	1 c. fresh mushrooms, sliced
1/2 c. flour	parsley for garnish

Mix salt, pepper and flour together in a shallow dish. Coat the chicken with the seasoned flour. Melt the butter and oil in a large dutch oven, and over medium high heat, brown the chicken. Add the sauce and cook the chicken over medium heat for 1 hour, or until tender. Add the mushrooms and cook for an additional 5 minutes. Place the chicken on a serving platter, pour the sauce around it, and garnish with parsley.

MARENGO SAUCE

1/4 c. butter	1 c. white wine
1/4 c. turnip, chopped	2 c. water
1 T. onion, minced	1/2 c. tomatoes, chopped
1/4 c. carrot, chopped	1 tsp. salt
1/4 c. flour	1/4 tsp. freshly ground pepper

Melt the butter in a large skillet and add the onion, carrot, and turnip. Sauté for 5 minutes. Next add the flour, salt and pepper; cook until the roux has turned light brown. Gradually add the water and tomatoes, and cook for 5 minutes. Strain.

MACARONI A LA ITALIENNE.

3/4 c. macaroni, uncooked   1 1/2 c. tomato sauce
1/2 onion   1/2 c. grated Parmesan cheese
2 tsp. butter   2 T. red wine

Place the macaroni, onion, and butter in a medium pot of boiling water. Cook until the macaroni is barely tender; about 15 minutes. Drain, and return the macaroni to the pot. Add the tomato sauce, cheese, and wine; heat through and serve.

TOMATO SAUCE

1 3/4 c. crushed tomatoes   1/4 tsp. salt
1/4 c. onion, chopped   1/2 tsp. freshly ground pepper
2 tsp. butter   1/2 tsp. parsley
2 T. flour   1/2 tsp. oregano

In a large skillet, cook the tomatoes and onions over medium heat until lightly browned. Strain and set aside. Add the butter and flour to the skillet and cook over medium heat for 2-3 minutes. Gradually stir in the tomato sauce and cook until slightly thickened. Add the seasonings.

PORK ROAST WITH APPLE SAUCE.

3-4 lb. boneless pork roast	1/4 tsp. freshly ground pepper
1/2 tsp. salt	1/4 c. flour
applesauce	

Sprinkle the roast with the salt and pepper. Next, dredge it in the flour. Place the pork in a roasting pan, fat side up. Bake, uncovered, for 2 to 2 1/2 hours at 325°. A meat thermometer should register 170° when the roast is done. Allow to stand for 15 minutes before serving. Arrange on a serving platter or plates and serve with applesauce.

APPLE SAUCE

8 tart apples	1 c. water
2/3 c. sugar	1" strip of a lemon rind

Peel, core and chop the apples. Place them in a medium stock pot; add the remaining ingredients and cook, covered, over medium low heat for 10 minutes. The apples should be very tender when done. Remove the lemon rind and mash.

BEEF A LA MODE.

Before you pass this recipe by, let me assure you that none of the ingredients include ice cream. A la mode simply means on the top.

4 lb. round roast	1/4 tsp. salt
8 pieces salt pork or bacon	1/4 tsp. freshly ground pepper
1/2 c. flour	1 sprig parsley
1/4 c. butter or margarine	1 bay leaf
1/3 c. turnip, diced	1 c. white wine
1/3 c. carrots, diced	Water, enough to halfway
1/3 c. onion, diced	cover roast
1/3 c. celery, diced	

Using a knife, make 8 slits horizontally in the meat. Place the pieces of salt pork or bacon into the slits. Season the meat with the salt and pepper, then dredge through the flour. In a large dutch oven, over medium heat, melt the butter or margarine. Brown the roast on all sides.

Add the remaining ingredients to the pan; be sure to put everything around the roast, not on it. Cover and cook over low heat for 4 hours. Do not allow the water to boil. When the roast is tender, remove and place on a serving platter. Strain the liquid, set aside.

In the same pan, melt 4 T. butter or margarine, add 4 T. flour and cook for 3-4 minutes, or until golden. Gradually add the reserved liquid and whisk for 5 minutes or until thick. Season with salt and pepper to taste. Pour the gravy over the roast or serve on the side.

SUGAR PEAS.

3 c. shelled tender sweet peas   6 T. butter or margarine,
7-8 quarts water   cut into pieces
8 tsp. salt   salt and pepper to taste
1/2 T. sugar

Place the water and salt in a large pot and bring to a boil. Add the peas and allow the water to come back to the boil. Gently boil, uncovered, for 7 minutes. Test the peas to check for firmness. If you like your peas more tender, continue boiling and check them again frequently.

Drain immediately, place the peas back in the pot and add the salt, pepper and sugar. Roll the peas around to evenly coat. Place in a serving bowl and place the cut up butter over the peas. Serve.

LEMON CAKE.

3/4 c. shortening   4 tsp. baking powder
1 1/2 c. sugar   1/2 tsp. salt
3 eggs   1/2 c. lemon juice
grated rind of 1 lemon   1/4 c. orange juice
3 c. sifted flour   1/2 c. milk

Cream the shortening and sugar together in a large bowl; beat until light and fluffy. Add eggs, one at a time, mixing thoroughly after each addition. Stir in the lemon rind and mix well.

In a small bowl, sift the flour, baking powder, and salt two times. Alternating with the juices and milk, add the flour to the shortening and sugar. Mix until thoroughly combined; about 2 minutes. Grease and line two 9-inch cake pans with waxed paper. Pour the batter into the pans and bake at 350° for 35-40 minutes or until done. Test with a toothpick. Cool the cake in pans for 10 minutes. Turn out onto cake cooling racks. Once the cake has completely cooled, fill and frost with whipped cream.*

See recipe on page 196.

GERMAN PANCAKES.

1 c. flour   1/4 tsp. salt
1 c. milk   3 T. butter
4 eggs, beaten

Combine all the ingredients together in a large bowl. Beat about 3 minutes, and then allow the batter to rest for 20 minutes.

Heat and 8" or 9" skillet that does not stick. Melt the butter over medium high heat, and when it bubbles, add 1/2 cup of the batter. Cook for 2 minutes and then gently flip the pancake over. Cook for an additional minute. You may need to adjust the heat to prevent burning the pancakes. Repeat this process until you have used all the batter. Serve with jam or powdered sugar. Makes 6.

CITY ITEMS

Notice.

German Pancakes every Saturday morning at the Russ House.

Attention A. O. U. W.

Tombstone Epitaph, 1881

RUSS HOUSE.

Sunday Bill of Fare—4:30 p. m. Toughnut Time.

SOUPS.

Chicken, Consomme

FISH.

Trout a Le Huile de Olives.

BOILED.

Leg of Mutton, Caper Sauce,
Beef, Tomato Sauce,
Corned Beef.

ENTRIES.

Croquettes of Lamb, with Green Peas,
Braised Ham, Champagne Sauce,
Chicken Saute, with Mushrooms,
Corn Starch Fritters, Wine Sauce,
Veal Marengoe, with Rice,
Chicken Giblets Pie,

ROASTS.

Prime Beef, Ribs of Beef, Leg of Mutton,
Stuffed Lamb, Dressed Veal, Pork,
with Apple Sauce, Chicken.

VEGETABLES.

Corn, String Beans,
Tomatoes and
Mashed Potatoes.

PASTRY.

Pumpkin and Apple Pie and Jelly Cake.

PUDDING.

Cocoanut, Cream Sauce.

DESERT.

Grapes and Apples.

RELISHES.

Assorted.

Meals served in private rooms 50 cents.
The same dinner in courses 75 cents.
Five extra waiters wanted for the Sunday dinners.

Russ House Bill of Fare   *Daily Nugget, 1881*

143

BOILED BEEF WITH TOMATO SAUCE.

6-8 thick slices leftover beef
1 c. tomatoes, fresh
   or canned
1 bay leaf
6 peppercorns

2 tsp. sugar
1/2 tsp. salt
4 T. butter
4 T. flour
1 c. brown stock*

To reheat the leftover boiled beef, melt the butter in a large skillet over med. heat. Sauté for a few minutes to heat through.

Combine the tomatoes, bay leaf, peppercorns, and sugar in a medium saucepan. Boil for 15 to 20 minutes. Press through a sieve to strain. Add the brown stock; set aside. In a large skillet, melt the butter over medium heat and cook until it has browned. Add the flour and cook until it has browned too. Slowly add the boiled tomato sauce and stir to blend.

Arrange the beef on a serving platter or individual plates, and spoon the sauce over top.

*See recipe on page 136.

CHICKEN GIBLETS PIE.

3 T. butter	1 c. white wine
2 tsp. garlic, minced	2 T. Worcestershire sauce
2 tsp. onion, minced	2 c. water or chicken stock
1/2 tsp. salt	2 lb. chicken giblets
1/4 tsp. freshly ground pepper	2 pie crusts*, unbaked
3 T. flour	

Melt the butter in a large stockpot, add the garlic, onion, salt and pepper. Sauté over medium heat for about 5 minutes. Do not allow the garlic to brown or it will become bitter. Sprinkle the flour over the mixture and cook for 2-3 minutes. Stirring constantly, slowly add the wine. Next add the Worcestershire sauce, chicken stock, and giblets. Bring this to a boil, reduce the heat and simmer for 30 minutes, or until the giblets are tender.

Line an 8 x 11 baking pan with one crust, pour the giblets into the crust and cover with the second crust. Flute the edges, and make two or three holes to allow the steam to escape. Bake at 350° for 45 minutes or until the crust has browned.

*See recipe on page 146.

MASHED POTATOES.

5 lg. potatoes, peeled & cubed	1/4 tsp. onion powder
1/2 tsp. salt	1/4 tsp. freshly ground pepper
3 T. butter	1/3-1/2 c. milk or cream

Place the potatoes in a large pot of cold water; add salt and bring to a boil. Cook over high heat for 15-20 minutes, or until just tender. Immediately drain the potatoes and mash. Add the butter, onion powder, and pepper. Gradually add enough milk to reach a fluffy consistency.

Note: for a special treat, try adding 1/2 c. grated parmesan cheese or Romano cheese.

PIE CRUST.
(My family recipe)

This recipe has been closely guarded by my family for decades. My father gave it to me and he learned from his mother, Anna White-Teeter, and so on. I hope my Grandmother doesn't mind that I'm sharing the best pie crust recipe ever, with my readers. After all, if we don't pass it along, it may one day be lost forever. This recipe is so good that my husband's Aunt Alice always asks me to make her just the crust, with no filling to get in the way of its great taste.

2 1/2 c. flour	1 egg
1 1/2 tsp. baking powder	1/2 tsp. vinegar
1/2 tsp. salt	cold water
3/4 c. shortening	

Combine the flour, baking powder and salt in a large mixing bowl. Stir to combine with a wire whisk. Cut in the shortening with a pastry cutter and blend until the dough resembles crumbs.

Break the egg into a liquid measuring cup; beat lightly. Add the vinegar and enough water to measure 1/3 c. on the measuring cup. Stir well. Add this to the flour and shortening mixture. Stir only enough to moisten and combine. Over mixing will result in a tough crust. If the seems too wet, add a little more flour.

Divide the dough in half and roll out on a floured surface. Makes two 9-inch pie crusts.

Note: To make a sweeter crust, add 1 tablespoon of sugar and a 1/2 teaspoon of cinnamon to the flour mix. Also, cut this recipe in half to make a single crust.

PUMPKIN PIE.

2 c. pumpkin
3/4 c. honey
1/2 tsp. salt
3 eggs, beaten
1 tsp. cinnamon

1/2 freshly grated nutmeg
1 c. evaporated milk
1 single pie crust recipe*,
   unbaked

In a large bowl, combine all the ingredients, except for the milk. Mix well and stir in the milk. Continue stirring until completely blended. Pour into a 9-inch pie shell and bake at 375° for 45-50 minutes. The pie is done when a knife inserted comes out clean. Cool slightly before cutting.

*See recipe on page 146.

GRAND HOTEL.

Bill of Fare for Sunday, Oct. 23d, 4.30
p. m. Tough Nut Time.

SOUP.

Chicken Giblet.

FISH.

Salmon, Egg Sauce.

BOILED.

Beef, Herb Sauce.

ROAST.

Chicken, Mushroom Sauce. Pork, Beef.

ENTREES.

Chicken Potpie,
   Beef a la Mode,
      Chicken Giblets,
         Ham, Champagne Sauce,
            Apple Fritters, Wine Sauce.

VEGETABLES.

Sweet Potatoes,
   Mashed Potatoes,
            Turnips,
                  Corn.

PASTRY.

Currant and Blackberry Pie,
            Ice Cream and Cake.

For Sale;

A nice little house of two rooms, with

Grand Hotel Bill of Fare *Daily Nugget*, 1881

ROAST CHICKEN WITH MUSHROOM SAUCE.

4 lb. chicken, cleaned
1 small onion, quartered
1/2 stalk celery
1 T. butter, softened

3 sprigs parsley
1/2 tsp. salt
1/4 tsp. freshly ground pepper

Sprinkle the inside of the chicken with the salt and pepper. Stuff with the onion, celery and parsley. Tie up. Spread the butter all over the bird and place in a roasting pan. Bake in a 350° oven for 1 to 1 1/2 hours. Pierce the inside leg of the chicken, if the juices run clear, then it's done. Remove the chicken and the juices from the pan. Allow the chicken to rest for 15 minutes before carving. Meanwhile, make the following sauce:

MUSHROOM SAUCE

1 c. fresh mushrooms, minced
2 T. green onions, chopped
1 T. butter
1 T. oil
1/2 c. dry white wine

1 c. brown stock*
1 T. tomato puree
2 T. butter, cut into bits
3 T. parsley, chopped

In a medium skillet sauté the mushrooms and onions in 1 T. of melted butter and oil, for 5 minutes. Add the wine and boil until almost completely evaporated. Whisk in the brown stock and tomato puree and simmer for 5 additional minutes. Remove from the heat and stir in the butter bits and parsley. Arrange the chicken on a serving platter and pour the sauce over the chicken. Garnish with fresh chopped green onions. Serves 4.

*See recipe on page 136.

HAM, CHAMPAGNE SAUCE.

This recipe is a good way to serve leftover ham. If you are using leftovers, skip to the champagne sauce.

5-7 lb. ham	whole cloves, about 30
1/2 c. brown sugar	depending on ham size
1/2 c. white wine	

Score the ham 1/4" deep and 1" apart. Place the ham in a baking pan, fat side up. Mix the brown sugar and wine in a small bowl and spread over the ham, reserving some of the mixture.. Push the cloves into the ham where you have scored it. Bake a 350° for 3 1/2 hours, basting occasionally with the sugar mixture. Check with a meat thermometer to ensure doneness. Slice the ham and serve with the following sauce:

CHAMPAGNE SAUCE

1/4 c. butter	6 peppercorns
1/4 c. carrot, chopped	5 T. flour
1/4 c. onion, sliced	2 c. beef stock
1 bay leaf	1/2 c. champagne
1 sprig thyme	1 T. powdered sugar
1/4 c. chopped fresh parsley	

Melt the butter in a large saucepan over medium heat. Sauté the vegetables and seasonings until lightly browned. Add the flour and cook until it starts to brown as well. Gradually add the stock and cook until slightly thickened. Strain the sauce and discard the vegetables. Return the sauce to the heat and cook for 5 minutes. Add the champagne and sugar; heat through and serve.

CHICKEN GIBLET SOUP.

1 turnip, sliced	Giblets of 1 chicken, chopped
1 onion, sliced	4 1/2 c. water
1 carrot, sliced	1/4 tsp. freshly ground pepper
1 T. butter or margarine	1/2 tsp. salt
1/4 c. flour	egg yolks, hard boiled

Sauté the vegetables in one tablespoon of butter in dutch oven over medium high heat until tender. Add the flour and giblets and cook until giblets brown. Add the water and simmer for 4-5 hours. Next add the salt and pepper.

When serving the soup, place an egg yolk in the bowl, and spoon the soup over it. Makes 1 quart.

BOILED BEEF WITH HERB SAUCE.

6-8 thick slices leftover beef	1/2 tsp. tarragon, crushed
1 T. butter	1/2 tsp. thyme
2 c. white sauce*	

To reheat the leftover boiled beef, melt the butter in a large skillet over medium heat. Sauté for a few minutes to heat through.

Combine the white sauce, tarragon and thyme; mix well. Arrange the beef on a serving platter or individual plates, and spoon the herb sauce over top. Garnish with a sprig of fresh thyme.

*See recipe on page 132.

Note: If you don't have tarragon and thyme, try substituting any green herb you like.

APPLE FRITTERS, SHERRY WINE SAUCE.

3/4 c. brandy or rum
1 1/3 c. flour, sifted
1/4 tsp. salt
2 tsp. baking powder
shortening for frying

2 T. sugar
1 egg
2/3 c. milk
4 apples

Core and peel the apples. Slice the apples about 1/8" thickness and place in a shallow container. Pour the brandy or rum over the apples and set aside for at least one half hour. In a medium size bowl, sift dry ingredients together. Add the egg and milk; blend well. The batter should be thick enough to coat the apple slices. Adjust the thickness of the batter with additional milk. In a frying pan, over medium high heat, add enough shortening to come up 2 inches in the pan.

While the shortening is heating up, drain the apples (reserve the brandy for use in sauce) and pat dry. Once the oil gets hot enough, dip the apples into the batter. Drop gently into the oil and fry 2-3 minutes or until golden. Remove from the oil and drain on a paper towel. Arrange on a serving platter, dust with confectioner's sugar and serve with sherry wine sauce.

SHERRY WINE SAUCE

1/2 c. butter, softened
1 c. powdered sugar

3 T. sherry
1/8 tsp. freshly grated nutmeg

In a medium bowl, whip the butter until light and fluffy. Gradually add the sugar, sherry, and nutmeg. Blend well.

CURRANT PIE.

1/4 c. flour	1 c. currants
2/3 c. sugar	2 egg yolks, beaten
1/3 c. honey	2 T. water
1 single pie crust*, unbaked	

Combine the flour, sugar and honey in a large bowl. Add the egg yolks and water; stir to combine. Wash the currants and remove the stems. (This should be done before measuring them.) Add the currants to the egg mixture and stir to ensure that the currants are coated evenly.

Pour into a 9-inch pie pan. Bake at 325° for 35 minutes. Remove the pie from the oven and cover with meringue. Return to the oven and bake until the meringue turns light brown; about 5 minutes. Allow to cool before cutting.

MERINGUE

3 egg whites	1/2 tsp. lemon juice or
3 T. powdered sugar	lemon extract

Beat the egg whites in a medium bowl until soft peaks form. Slowly add the sugar and lemon while beating constantly. Whip until stiff peaks form. You should be able to put some in a spoon and turn it upside down without the meringue falling off.

*See recipe on page 146.

ALMOND CAKE.
(Pain de Genes)

2/3 c. almonds	2 eggs
1/4 c. flour	1 tsp. vanilla extract
1/2 c. sugar	3 T. dark rum
1/2 c. butter or margarine	Confectioner's sugar for dusting

Preheat oven to 350°. Mix the almonds with 1/3 c. of the sugar and grind until fine. (A food processor will do this quickly.) Add the flour and mix well; set aside. Cream the sugar and butter in a large bowl. Add the eggs, 1 at a time, combining well after each addition. Next add the vanilla and rum; beat until completely mixed. Add the almond mixture and blend until smooth. Butter and slightly flour an 8" or 9" cake pan. Line the bottom of the pan with parchment or wax paper. Pour the batter in the pan; please note that it will only come up a quarter of the way on the pan.

Bake for 30-35 minutes or until golden and pulls away from the sides of the pan. Cool completely; dust the top with confectioner's sugar. Garnish with fresh berries and mint leaves. Serves 8.

BLACKBERRY PIE.

This recipe brings backs memories of my childhood when my sister and I would visit my Aunt Anna's house where we picked fresh blackberries and raspberries. We'd bring them back to her, and a few hours later, we were enjoying a piece of freshly baked pie. What a treat!

3 c. fresh blackberries	2 T. lemon juice
1 c. sugar	1 T. butter, cut into pieces
2 T. flour	2 pie crusts

Combine the berries, sugar, flour, and lemon juice together in a large bowl. Gently toss the mixture to evenly coat the berries. Pour into a lined 9" pie pan, dot with butter, and cover with the second pie crust. Cut 3 or 4 holes in the crust to allow the steam to escape. Bake at 350° for 35-40 minutes, or until the berries are tender. Allow to cool 30 minutes before cutting. Serve with whipped cream and freshly grated nutmeg.

OCCIDENTAL RESTAURANT.

Sunday Bill of Fare - October 30.

SOUPS.

Chicken Giblet and Crot au pot.

FISH.

Baracauta su Buerre et Noir, and Salt
Cod, with Pork scraps.

BOILED.

~~Leg of Lamb, sauce Oyster,~~ Corned Beef
and Cabbage.
Leg of Pork. Pickle sauce.

RELIEVES

Round of Beef, a la Financier,
Lobster Salad, en Mayonaise.

ROASTS.

Loin of Beef,
Loin of Lamb,
Loin of Veal,
Turkey, Cranberry sauce,
Chicken;
Sucking Pig,
Leg of Pork, Apple Sauce.

ENTREES.

La petite pate d' Saumon, a la Straus-
burg.
Sevaillle d' Agneau, a la Poulette.
Lobster Curry, in bordera of Cocoanut.
Riz d' Bean, a la Espagnol.
Tirmoul of Rice, with Currant Jelly
Peach Chocolate, glace a la Empereur.

PASTRY.

Custard, Lemon, Squash and Apple Pies.

DESERT.

English Plum Pudding, Brandy sauce.
The wonder of the world! A meal in
Tombstone like this for 50 cts. Come and
see.

Occidental Restaurant Bill of Fare

Tombstone Epitaph, 1881

CROT AU POT.

4 c. consomme*, warmed   10-12 slices French bread
Parmesan cheese

Slice the bread 3/4" thickness and place on a greased baking sheet. Bake at 325° for 25 minutes. Put two or three slices of bread in the soup bowl. Ladle the consommé over the bread and sprinkle with cheese.

See recipe on page 135.

LOBSTER CURRY IN BORDERS OF COCONUT.

1 1/2 c. white sauce*   1/2 tsp. salt
1 1/2 tsp. curry powder   1/4 tsp. freshly ground pepper
2 tsp. lemon juice   2-lb. lobster, cooked & chopped
coconut

Place the white sauce in a large saucepan and add the remaining ingredients, except the coconut. Stir to combine, and cook over medium heat until warmed.

Place the coconut along the edge of a round serving platter to form a circle, then spoon the lobster in the center. Serve warm.

See recipe on page 132.

LEMON PIE.

Lemon Pie is always a crowd pleaser, and one of my favorites.

1 1/4 c. sugar	3 T. butter
5 1/3 T. cornstarch	4 T. lemon juice
1 1/2 c. hot water	1 1/2 T. grated lemon rind
3 eggs, separated	1 pie crust*, pre-baked

Combine the sugar, cornstarch, and water in a large saucepan. Cook over medium high heat until the mixture begins to boil and become thick. Remove from the heat. In a small bowl, beat the egg yolks until thick and lemon colored. Gradually add 3 tablespoons of the cooked mixture to the egg yolks and stir well. Now add the egg yolks to the saucepan and incorporate. Cook this over medium high heat for about 1 minute, stirring constantly. Add in the butter, lemon juice, and lemon rind. Pour into a pie shell and top with meringue. Bake at 375° for 10-15 minutes or until the meringue becomes golden.

MERINGUE

3 egg whites	1 tsp. lemon juice
3/4 c. sugar	

Beat the egg whites in a large bowl until soft peaks form. Gradually beat in the sugar and lemon juice until stiff peaks have formed.

*See recipe on page 146.

OLD ENGLISH PLUM PUDDING.

This recipe will require some patience and a lot of cooking time. It's not probably something you would make often, but everyone should try it once to experience the food of our ancestors.

1 lb. suet	1/3 c. citron
3/4 lb. bread crumbs	1/3 c. candied lemon peel
1 lb. sugar	1/3 c. candied orange peel
1 lb. flour	6 eggs, beaten
1 lb. raisins	1 qt. milk
1 lb. currants	

Mix suet, bread and sugar, in a large bowl; combine well. Next add the flour, fruits and peel. Lastly, add the eggs and milk and stir well.

Fill several small ramekins or oven proof dishes. Tie a wet non-flammable cloth around each dish. Set in shallow pan filled with water. Cook in simmering water for 10 hours. Check the water level; if needed, add additional boiling water. The pudding may be reheated by boiling again. Serve with hard brandy sauce.

HARD BRANDY SAUCE

1/2 c. butter	1 tsp. vanilla extract
1 c. powdered sugar	2 T. brandy
Fresh grated nutmeg	

Cream the butter and sugar together in a medium bowl until light and fluffy. Stir in the vanilla and brandy. Mix well. Grate a few grains of nutmeg on the top.

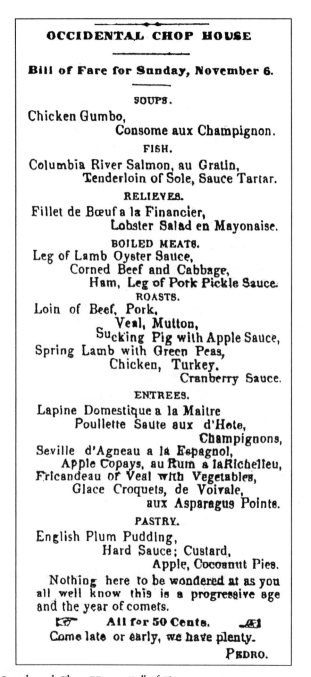

OCCIDENTAL CHOP HOUSE

Bill of Fare for Sunday, November 6.

SOUPS.
Chicken Gumbo,
Consome aux Champignon.

FISH.
Columbia River Salmon, au Gratin,
Tenderloin of Sole, Sauce Tartar.

RELIEVES.
Fillet de Bœuf a la Financier,
Lobster Salad en Mayonaise.

BOILED MEATS.
Leg of Lamb Oyster Sauce,
Corned Beef and Cabbage,
Ham, Leg of Pork Pickle Sauce.

ROASTS.
Loin of Beef, Pork,
Veal, Mutton,
Sucking Pig with Apple Sauce,
Spring Lamb with Green Peas,
Chicken, Turkey.
Cranberry Sauce.

ENTREES.
Lapine Domestique a la Maitre
Poullette Saute aux d'Hote,
Champignons,
Seville d'Agneau a la Espagnol,
Apple Copays, au Rum a laRichelieu,
Fricandeau of Veal with Vegetables,
Glace Croquets, de Voivale,
aux Asparagus Points.

PASTRY.
English Plum Pudding,
Hard Sauce; Custard,
Apple, Cocoanut Pies.

Nothing here to be wondered at as you
all well know this is a progressive age
and the year of comets.

☞ **All for 50 Cents.** ☜
Come late or early, we have plenty.

PEDRO.

Occidental Chop House Bill of Fare   Tombstone Epitaph, 1881

CHICKEN GUMBO SOUP.

You can see the influence of the Occidental's new cook, Alvan Young, from this recipe. Prior to working in Tombstone and at the Occidental, Alvan had been a cook on a Mississippi River steamboat.

2-3 lb. chicken	1 tsp. cayenne pepper sauce
2 qts. water	1 tsp. thyme
2 c. okra, sliced thick	1 T. parsley
1/2 tsp. salt	1/4 c. dry bread crumbs
1/4 tsp. freshly ground pepper	1 T. butter or margarine
1 T. Worcestershire sauce	

In a large dutch oven, boil the chicken in the water until completely cooked and tender, about an hour. Remove the chicken and de-bone. Skim off excess fat from the chicken stock and add the okra and cook over medium high heat for 15 minutes. Add the chicken and remaining ingredients, stir and heat through. Serve with crusty French bread.

CONSOMMÉ AUX CHAMPIGNONS
(Consommé with Mushrooms)

1/2 lb. mushrooms, sliced   4 c. consommé*

Place the mushrooms and 1 cup of the consommé on a large sauté pan and allow to boil over medium heat for about 10 minutes. Strain the sauce and remove the mushrooms. Add the sauce back to all the consommé, and garnish with mushrooms.

See recipe on page 135.

BOILED LEG OF LAMB, OYSTER SAUCE.

5 lb. leg of lamb	water
salt	

Place the lamb in a large dutch oven. Add enough cold water, (be sure to measure it) to cover the lamb. Remove the lamb and add 1 1/2 teaspoons of salt for every 4 cups of water you added. Bring this to a boil. Put the lamb into the boiling water and allow it to come back to a low boil. Reduce the heat to medium and cook for 1 1/2 hours or until a meat thermometer registers 160° (well done). Remove from the water and allow to rest for 20 minutes before serving. Arrange on a serving platter and pour the oyster sauce around the slices.

OYSTER SAUCE

2 pts. oysters	2 c. milk
1/2 c. butter	1 tsp. salt
1/2 c. flour	1/2 tsp. freshly ground pepper

Wash and shuck the oysters, being sure to reserve the oyster liquor. Strain the oyster liquor, set aside. Melt the butter in a deep frying pan over medium heat. Once the butter has melted, add the flour and cook for 3 minutes. Whisking constantly, gradually pour in the milk and oyster liquor; stir well. Add the salt, pepper and oysters. Allow this to cook until the edges of the oysters being to curl. Remove from heat.

LOBSTER SALAD.

The Tombstone Epitaph also printed a recipe for Lobster Salad in 1890; I have listed it below for you.

2 c. lobster, cooked	1/2 tsp. salt
& chopped fine	1/4 tsp. freshly ground pepper
1/4 c. lettuce, shredded	1/2 tsp. mustard

Place all the ingredients in a large bowl and combine well. Serve on a bed of lettuce with toast points. To make toast points, toast slices of bread and cut into triangles. Serves 2-3.

LOBSTER SALAD

Plunge two lobsters in boiling water and let cook half an hour; take the center of six heads of lettuce and three hard boiled eggs; break off the shells of the lobsters. Take out the flesh and cut in small pieces; put salad in a bowl and season with salt and pepper, oil and vinegar; wash the lettuce, tear in pieces, mix with the lobster and cover with mayonnaise dressing.

LAPINE DOMESTIQUE (RABBIT) A LA CHASSUER.

1 rabbit, cut up	1/4 tsp. freshly ground pepper
1 tsp. thyme	1/2 tsp. oil
1 tsp. powdered bay leaf	2 T. butter
1/2 tsp. salt	

Combine the thyme, bay leaf, salt and pepper in a small bowl. Rub the seasonings over the rabbit pieces. Next, melt the butter and oil over medium high heat in a large frying pan. Once the butter has melted, add the rabbit and sauté until golden brown on all sides.

Arrange the rabbit pieces on a serving platter and pour the Chasseur sauce over them. Sprinkle with freshly chopped parsley. If you can't get rabbit, try using chicken instead.

CHASSEUR SAUCE

1/2 lb. mushrooms, sliced	1/4 tsp. salt
2 T. butter	1/8 tsp. freshly ground pepper
1 T. oil	1/2 tsp. tarragon
1/4 c. shallots, minced	1/2 c. white wine
1 c. tomatoes, chopped	1/2 c. thickened brown stock*
1 clove garlic, minced	

Sauté the mushrooms in the melted butter and oil for 5 minutes over medium heat; add the shallots and cook for a minute more. Next, add the tomatoes, garlic, and seasonings; simmer for 5 minutes. Pour the wine and brown stock over the tomato mixture and boil for 5 minutes, or until the sauce has thickened. This sauce may be used in a variety of dishes.

*See recipe on page 136.

CROQUETTES DE VOVAILLE, AUX ASPARAGUS POINTS.

(Chicken Croquettes with Asparagus Points)

1 3/4 c. chicken, cooked & minced	1/4 tsp. minced onion
1/2 tsp. salt	1 tsp. parsley, chopped
1/4 tsp. freshly ground pepper	1 c. white sauce
1/4 tsp. celery salt	dry bread crumbs for coating
1 tsp. lemon juice	3 eggs, beaten
	oil for frying

Mix the first seven ingredients together in a bowl, stir well. Add enough of the white sauce to moisten the mixture, but do not allow it to become too soft. Form the mixture into desired shapes, such as cones, balls, cylinders, etc. Roll the shapes in the bread crumbs first, then in the eggs, and then back in the bread crumbs.

Gently place the croquettes in the hot oil and cook until they are golden brown. Drain on a towel. Arrange croquettes on a serving platter and garnish with asparagus points. See page 132 for asparagus recipe.

Note: this recipe would also work well with leftover turkey.

SQUASH PIE.

Squash Pie is one of my husband's favorites. This recipe is as close to his Grandmother's, Helen Sweet, as I could get without having her recipe. He never liked pumpkin pie and always talked about her squash pie, so one Thanksgiving I came up with this recipe and he said it reminded him of Grandma's.

1 c. sugar	1 c. cooked & mashed squash
3/4 tsp. salt	or zucchini
1 tsp. cinnamon	3 eggs, beaten
1 tsp. freshly grated nutmeg	1 c. evaporated milk
	1 pie crust*, unbaked

Add the ingredients, except for pie crust, in the order given. Be sure to stir thoroughly after each addition. Pour into a 9" pie pan and bake at 450° for 10 minutes, reduce the temperature to 350° and bake 40 minutes more. The pie will be done when a knife inserted in, comes out clean.

*See recipe on page 146.

CUSTARD PIE.

3 eggs	1/8 tsp. salt
3 T. sugar	1 1/4 c. milk
nutmeg, freshly grated	1 8" pie crust

In a large bowl, beat the eggs. Add the sugar, salt and milk; whip until light and fluffy.

Pour the custard into the pie crust and sprinkle the top with freshly grated nutmeg. Bake at 450° for 10 minutes, reduce the heat to 350° and continue cooking for an additional 50 minutes or until a knife inserted comes out clean.

Allow to cool completely before cutting. Chilling the pie enhances the flavors.

RUSS HOUSE.

Dinner Bill of Fare.

TOMBSTONE, Sunday, Nov. 27.

SOUPS.

Chicken and Consomme Royal

FISH.

Baked Salmon, Stuffed a la Richelieu.

BOILED.

Leg of Mutton, Caper Sauce,

Westphalia Ham,

Corned Beef.

ENTREES.

Braised Ribs of Beef, a la Piedmontais.

Chicken Pot Pie;

Rice Cake, with Jelly and Sherry Wine Sauce,

Saute of Lamb and Green Peas,

Curry of Chicken Giblets and Rice.

ROASTS.

Ribs of Beef, Prime Beef Stuffed.

Mutton Lamb. Veal.

Pork with Apple Sauce.

VEGETABLES.

Corn. Sugar Peas; Tomatoes.

Sweet and Mashed Potatoes.

PASTRY.

Assorted Pies and Lemon Drops.

PUDDINGS.

New York Plum, Hard Sauce, Lemon Flavor.

DESSERT.

Apples and Walnuts.

Tea and Coffee. Or Wines.

N. B.—Guests inviting friends will please give notice in the office. All meals or fruits sent to rooms will be charged extra. Children occupying seats at the first table will be charged full price.

☞ The proprietors request that Guests

Russ House Bill of Fare   *Daily Nugget, 1881*

CONSOMMÉ ROYAL.

3 egg yolks, beaten
1 whole egg, beaten
1/2 c. consomme*

1/8 tsp. salt
1/8 tsp. nutmeg
pinch cayenne pepper

Combine above ingredients and beat well. Pour into a small buttered mold. Place in a hot pan of water and bake at 350° for 15-20 minutes or until firm. Cool and cut into fancy shapes. Garnish consommé with a few before serving.

* See recipe on page 135.

CHICKEN POT PIE.

1 chicken, stewed & deboned
2 T. butter or margarine
3/4 tsp. salt
1/2 tsp. freshly ground pepper
1 T. flour

2 c. chicken stock
1 double crust pie recipe*, unbaked
6 medium potatoes, diced & boiled

Place the chicken, butter, salt and pepper in a large stock pot. Once the butter has melted add the flour and cook for 2 minutes; stirring constantly. Slowly add the chicken stock; stir until lightly thickened. Remove from the heat.

Line a deep dish pie pan with first crust. Put in a layer of chicken and then a layer of potatoes; repeating until the top is reached. Pour the gravy over the chicken and potatoes; cover with the second crust. Bake at 350° for 30 minutes or until crust is golden.

*See recipe on page 146.

SALMON, BAKED A LA RICHELEAU

This is not a low calorie fish recipe, but it's really delicious and one of my favorites in this book. If you're concerned about the fat, omit the sauce, it's good without it, too.

2 lb. salmon, cut into serving pieces	3 eggs, beaten
	1 c. dry bread crumbs
1/2 tsp. salt	4 T. butter
1/4 tsp. freshly ground pepper	1 T. oil

Season the salmon with salt and pepper. Dip the salmon pieces in the beaten eggs and then in the bread crumbs. Melt the butter and oil in an ovenproof skillet (cast iron works great), over high heat. When the butter bubbles, add the salmon and quickly brown on both sides. Place the skillet in a 450° oven and bake for about 5-8 minutes, depending on the thickness of the salmon. When done, a fork should pierce the center of the salmon easily.

Place the salmon on a platter and serve with Maitre d' Hotel sauce.

MAITRE D' HOTEL SAUCE

1 c. butter	1/8 tsp. cayenne pepper
1 tsp. chopped parsley	1/4 tsp. salt
juice of 1 lemon	

Combine all the ingredients in a medium sauce pan and cook over medium low heat until the butter has melted. Allow to simmer for 1 minute.

CREAM PIE #1.

1 c. sugar	2 c. milk, scalded
1/3 c. flour	1 tsp. vanilla extract
1/4 tsp. salt	1/2 tsp. lemon extract
2 eggs, well beaten	3 8" pie crusts* (pre-baked)

In a large metal bowl, combine dry ingredients; stir in eggs and milk, stir to combine. Place the bowl over a pot of simmering water (a double boiler may be substituted). Cook the mixture for 15 minutes, stirring constantly until thickened; check your heat as you do not want to scramble the eggs. Cool mixture and add the flavorings.

Put a 1/2 cup of the cream filling into 1 pie crust. Place another crust on top of this one. Fill with another 1/2 cup of cream filling. Add the third and final pie crust to the top and add remaining filling on top. Dust with powdered sugar and garnish with mint leaves and berries.

The pie should be served immediately. Do not allow it to sit too long or it will become soggy.

See recipe on page 146.

'-Joot level, in
isive body of
the combina-
progresses, a,
been struck
not been fully
ug about the
nth as last.

continue
accounts
w nothing but
quite a large
ng formation
ledge, there is
it is perma-
ide bonanza.

irly won the
f all that its
In the east-
about the only
body remains
etofore. The
ions than ever
a body. The
egular month-
o doubt be in-
,000 when the
y have in cou-

i-enne They
f it were not

way to lessen
trouble stings
sped and not

not handsome
learned at for-
uever be hand-
rich in this

OCCIDENTAL RESTAURANT.

Sunday, November 27th, 1881.

SOUPS.

Chicken Giblet,   Brunoise.

FISH.

Salmon au Pomme 'd Terre Croquette,
Codfish. Creme a la Creme.

RELIEVES.

Fillet 'd Beau, aux Petite Fois,
Turkey Hash with Dropped Eggs,

BOILED.

Russian River Bacon, with Cabbage,
Leg of Lamb, Oyster sauce,
Leg of Pork. Pickle Sauce,
Westphalia Ham.

ROAST.

Loin of Beef,
Stuffed Shoulder of Mutton,
Leg of Pork. Apple sauce,
Spring Lamb, Mint sauce,
Ribs of Beef, with Horse raddish,
Turkey, with Cramberry sauce,
Westphalia Ham, Champagne sauce,
and Chicken.

ENTREES.

Vol au Bent des Fritters, a la Maryland,
Baritaria Shrimps Curried, East Indian
style.
Salmes of Teal Duck, with Spanish Olives,
Charlotte des Pommes, a la Prince Albert,
Pidion d'Poulette, au Petite Pois.

PASTRY.

Apple, Mince, Peach, Plum,
Custard Pies.

DESSERT.

Assorted small Pastry,
Jenny Lind Pudding, Cream sauce.

We will have the above, and serve the
same for 50 cents.   A. PETRO.

Wanted,
A second hand baby carriage. Inquire

beveug
This pap
Seventh st
streets, in
one of the
houses in
week. or
rates.

Wells, F
ing his bu
pounds. Yo

Crea
Of ai! t
my life to
York to
which con
northern s
as the mo
misgiving
curves.
hurled by
the Tasma
less rapid
way roun
wooded h
parently
occasional
bends tha
dow and
locomotiv
the experi
rather th
Tasmania
tion hithe
therefor.
otherwise
seeins to
centric a
the win
run across
us to Hol
thetic rea
doped the
here, wo
general s

Occidental Restaurant Bill of Fare   *Daily Nugget, 1881*

CODFISH, CREME A LA CREME.

2 lb. codfish
1 c. white sauce*
1 T. parsley
1/2 c. dry bread crumbs

1/2 slice onion
1/2 tsp. salt
1/4 tsp. freshly ground pepper

Place enough water to come up a 1/2" in a large skillet. Add a slice of lemon, a few peppercorns and a bay leaf. Bring this to a boil. Add the uncooked fish, cover, and reduce heat to simmer and cook for 10 minutes. This fish will be done when a fork can easily pierce the fish. Allow to cool.

In a small bowl, flake the fish with a fork. Place half of the fish on an oven proof platter. Add the parsley, onion, salt, and pepper. Next pour half white sauce over the fish. Layer the rest of the fish on top and repeat the process. Sprinkle the top with the bread crumbs and bake at 375° for 15-20 minutes, or until the top has browned. Serves 4.

See recipe on page 132.

TURKEY HASH WITH DROPPED EGGS.

It appears that even back in the 1880s they found unique ways to use the leftover Thanksgiving turkey. If you note the date of the bill of fare from which this recipe came, you will see that it is shortly after Thanksgiving. Give this recipe a try with your next leftover turkey.

2 T. butter	1/2 tsp. salt
2 c. turkey, cooked	1/4 tsp. freshly ground pepper
& chopped	1/2 c. water or chicken stock
1 T. parsley	

Melt the butter in a large skillet over medium high heat. Add the remaining ingredients, in the order given. Cook for about 10 minutes, turning frequently. Pile the hash on a serving platter and garnish with dropped eggs.

DROPPED EGGS

1 tsp. salt	4 eggs
water	

Place the salt and water in a large sauce pan; bring to a boil. Gently break the eggs into the boiling water and reduce the heat to medium low, and simmer for 3 minutes. Drain the eggs and serve.

APPLE PIE.

4 or 5 green apples	1 tsp. lemon juice
1/3 c. sugar	1/8 tsp. salt
1/4 tsp. grated nutmeg	1 tsp. butter or margarine
1/8 tsp. grated lemon rind	1 double crust pie*, unbaked

Peel, core and cut apples into thin slices. Place the apples and the next five ingredients in a bowl. Mix to coat the apples evenly. Line the bottom of the pastry shell with the apples. Dot with butter and place crust over top, being sure to seal and flute the edges. Take a knife and cut a few small holes in the top of the crust for the steam to escape.

Bake at 350° for 40-45 minutes, or until apples are tender. Allow to cool slightly before cutting.

*See recipe on page 146.

CHARLOTTE DES POMMES.
(Apple Charlotte)

This is an especially tasty dessert and it's not as complicated as you might think. It's a great way to use not so fresh bread.

4 qts. apples, sliced 1/8"	3 T. butter
1/2 c. apricot preserves	1/4 c. dark rum
2/3 c. sugar	3/4 c. butter, melted
2 tsp. vanilla extract	12 slices bread, 1/4" thick

Place the peeled, sliced apples in a large skillet and cover. Cook over low heat for 20 minutes; stirring occasionally. The apples should be tender when done. When tender, add the preserves, sugar, 2 tablespoons of butter, and rum. Cook over high heat, stirring constantly, until the mixture begins to thicken. Add vanilla; remove from heat.

Remove the crusts from the bread. Cut some of the bread into pieces to fit the bottom and sides of your mold. Brown these in 1 tablespoon of butter, and put in the mold. Cut the remaining bread into 1/2" wide strips. Heavily brush the strips with the melted butter and line the mold with them. Make sure that each strip overlaps the other so there are no spaces in between.

Pour the apples into the mold and press down lightly. The apples should be mounded on top as they will settle when cooking. Trim off any uneven bread. Cover the top with additional buttered bread strips. Thoroughly brush the top again with melted butter. Place the mold on a baking sheet and bake at 425° for 30 minutes. Cool in the mold for 15 minutes. Turn out onto a serving platter by slowly lifting the mold off the charlotte. If the charlotte starts to collapse, set the mold down, and try again in 5 minutes. Brush the charlotte with the glaze. To make the glaze, boil 1/2 c. strained apricot jam, 3 T. dark rum, and 2 T. sugar, until thick. This dessert can be served hot or cold.

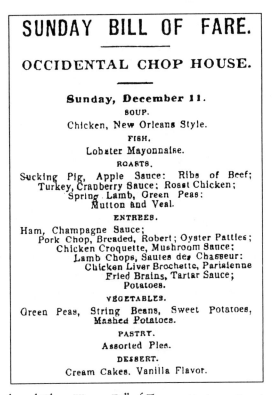

SUNDAY BILL OF FARE.

OCCIDENTAL CHOP HOUSE.

Sunday, December 11.

SOUP.

Chicken, New Orleans Style.

FISH.

Lobster Mayonnaise.

ROASTS.

Sucking Pig, Apple Sauce: Ribs of Beef;
Turkey, Cranberry Sauce; Roast Chicken;
Spring Lamb, Green Peas;
Mutton and Veal.

ENTREES.

Ham, Champagne Sauce;
Pork Chop, Breaded, Robert; Oyster Patties;
Chicken Croquette, Mushroom Sauce;
Lamb Chops, Sautes des Chasseur:
Chicken Liver Brochette, Parisienne
Fried Brains, Tartar Sauce;
Potatoes.

VEGETABLES.

Green Peas, String Beans, Sweet Potatoes,
Mashed Potatoes.

PASTRY.

Assorted Pies.

DESSERT.

Cream Cakes. Vanilla Flavor.

Occidental Chop House Bill of Fare   *Tombstone Epitaph*, 1881

PORK CUTLETS, SAUCE ROBERT.

4-6 pork cutlets, 1/2" thick	2 c. brown stock
1 T. butter	3 T. Dijon mustard
1 T. oil	2 T. parsley
1/2 onion, minced	1 c. dry white wine

Cook the cutlets over medium high heat in a large skillet until they are no loner pink inside; about 20 minutes. Remove the cutlets and place on a serving platter. Place the onions in the skillet and cook for 10 minutes, or until tender. Slowly add the wine and allow it to reduce to about 4 tablespoons. Add the brown stock and allow to simmer for 12 minutes. Remove from the heat and whisk in the mustard and parsley. Pour the sauce around the cutlets and garnish parsley sprigs.

175

MASHED POTATOES, FRENCH STYLE.

1 garlic head, separated	2 1/2 lbs. potatoes, peeled
4 T. butter or margarine	& cubed
2 T. flour	3 T. butter or margarine
1 c. milk, boiling	salt and white pepper to taste
1/4 tsp. salt	3-4 T. heavy cream
dash freshly ground pepper	4 T. parsley, minced

Place the garlic in a pot of boiling water; boil for 2 minutes. Drain. Peel the garlic; set aside. Put 4 T. butter and the garlic in a 4 quart saucepan, cover and slowly cook for 20 minutes, being sure not to brown the garlic. Add the flour and stir over low heat for 2 minutes. Again, do not brown. Remove the pan from the heat, add the milk, salt and pepper. Place back over high heat, stirring constantly for 1 minute. Puree the sauce in a blender.

In a large stockpot, cover the potatoes with water and boil until tender, about 20 minutes. When the potatoes can be pierced easily with a fork, they are done. Drain immediately. Mash the potatoes in the stockpot used for boiling. Place over medium heat and stir constantly until the potatoes coat the bottom of the pot. Remove from heat, mix in remaining butter, one tablespoon at a time. Add the salt and white pepper. Beat in the hot garlic sauce. Next, slowly add the cream, until desired consistency is reached. Add parsley and serve hot. Makes enough for 4-6 people.

STRING BEANS.

2 lbs. green string beans	1/4 tsp. salt
3 T. butter or margarine	1/8 tsp. freshly ground pepper

Boil the beans in 5 quarts of water. Cook for 6 to 8 minutes, or until tender. Drain the beans and run under cold water to stop the cooking process. Drain again. Sauté the cooked beans in the butter over medium high heat, stirring often to coat with butter. Season with salt and pepper. Serves 4.

SWEET POTATOES.

6 sweet potatoes   6 T. butter

Wash the potatoes and pat dry. Place on a baking sheet and bake at 375° for 40-45 minutes, or until tender. Slice lengthwise and spread the butter. Cinnamon and sugar may also be sprinkled on for additional sweetness.

PLUM PIE.

3 c. fresh plums, pitted   1/2 tsp. salt
1 c. sugar   2 pie crusts*, unbaked
2 T. flour   1 T. butter, cut into pieces
2 T. lemon juice

Combine all the ingredients, except for the pie crust and butter, in a large bowl. Pour this into a 9" pie pan, dot with the butter pieces and cover with second crust.

Bake at 450° for 10 minutes, reduce the temperature to 350° and bake an additional 35 minutes, or until the plums are tender.

*See recipe on page 146.

CREAM CAKE, VANILLA FLAVOR.

Note the cake description contains "vanilla flavor." This was done because the common flavoring of the time was lemon, not vanilla. Vanilla was not commonly used until much later. This was largely because is was not readily available.

2 eggs	1/2 tsp. salt
3/4 c. light cream	1/2 tsp. baking soda
1 1/2 c. flour	1 tsp. vanilla extract
2 1/2 tsp. baking powder	
1 c. sugar	

Combine eggs, cream and sugar in a large bowl and whip until light. In a smaller bowl, sift the flour, salt, baking soda and baking powder. Add the sifted ingredients and vanilla to the eggs and cream; mix well.

Pour the batter into a 9-inch cake pan that has been greased and floured. Bake at 350° for 25-30 minutes. Check with a toothpick for doneness. Allow the cake to cool in the pan for 5 minutes, then remove from the pan and cool completely on a cake rack. Once the cake has cooled, slice in half to make two layers, and fill with cream sauce.

CREAM SAUCE (DESSERT)

3/4 c. heavy cream	1/4 c. powdered sugar
1/4 c. milk	1/2 tsp. lemon or vanilla extract

Combine the cream and milk in a cold bowl and whip until stiff. Add the sugar and flavoring; stir well.

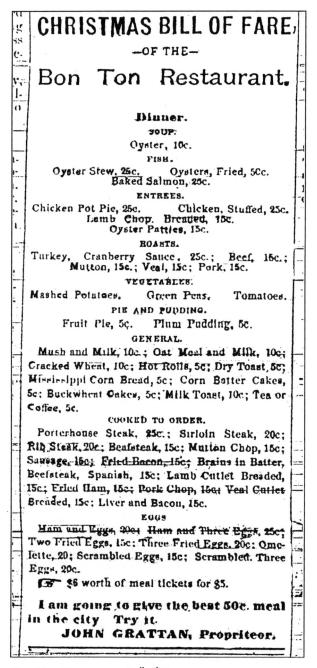

CHRISTMAS BILL OF FARE,

—OF THE—

Bon Ton Restaurant.

Dinner.

SOUP.
Oyster, 10c.

FISH.
Oyster Stew, 25c.   Oysters, Fried, 5Cc.
Baked Salmon, 25c.

ENTREES.
Chicken Pot Pie, 25c.   Chicken, Stuffed, 25c.
Lamb Chop. Breaded, 15c.
Oyster Pattles, 15c.

ROASTS.
Turkey, Cranberry Sauce, 25c.; Beef, 15c.;
Mutton, 15c.; Veal, 15c; Pork, 15c.

VEGETABLES.
Mashed Potatoes.   Green Peas.   Tomatoes.

PIE AND PUDDING.
Fruit Pie, 5c.   Plum Pudding, 5c.

GENERAL.
Mush and Milk, 10c.; Oat Meal and Milk, 10c.;
Cracked Wheat, 10c; Hot Rolls, 5c; Dry Toast, 5c;
Mississippi Corn Bread, 5c; Corn Batter Cakes,
5c; Buckwheat Cakes, 5c; Milk Toast, 10c; Tea or
Coffee, 5c.

COOKED TO ORDER.
Porterhouse Steak, 25c.; Sirloin Steak, 20c;
Rib Steak, 20c; Beafsteak, 15c; Mutton Chop, 15c;
Sausage, 15c; Fried Bacon, 15c; Brains in Batter,
Beefsteak, Spanish, 15c; Lamb Cutlet Breaded,
15c; Fried Ham, 15c; Pork Chop, 15c; Veal Cutlet
Breaded, 15c; Liver and Bacon, 15c.

EGGS
Ham and Eggs, 20c; Ham and Three Eggs, 25c;
Two Fried Eggs, 15c; Three Fried Eggs, 20c; Ome-
lette, 20; Scrambled Eggs, 15c; Scrambled Three
Eggs, 20c.

☞ $6 worth of meal tickets for $5.

I am going to give the best 50c. meal
in the city Try it.
JOHN GRATTAN, Proprietor.

Bon Ton Restaurant Bill of Fare   Tombstone Epitaph, 1881

OYSTER SOUP.

4 c. oysters	1 parsley sprig
3/4 c. water	1 small bay leaf
4 c. milk	1 slice of onion
1/3 c. butter or margarine	1 stalk celery
1/3 c. flour	salt & pepper to taste
1 tsp. mace	

Clean oysters and coarsely chop. Place in a large pot, add the water and bring to a boil over medium heat. Remove from heat and drain; reserving the oyster liquor. Set oysters aside in a bowl. In the same pot, melt the butter and add flour, stirring to make a roux. Add the reserved liquor and blend until smooth.

In a separate pot, scald the milk and remaining ingredients. Strain the milk into the thickened roux and mix until combined. Place the oysters in the pot and stir. Serve immediately. Garnish with fresh parsley sprig.

OYSTER STEW.

This stew is a "Monahan" family tradition on Christmas Eve. My in-laws always make oyster stew for dinner and then enjoy a variety of hors d'oeuvres with their family, friends, and neighbors.

1 qt. oysters	1/4 c. butter
3/4 c. water	1/2 tsp. salt
4 c. milk, scalded	

Place cleaned oysters in a large stock pot; add the water and slowly bring to a boil, until the oysters open. Strain, reserving the oyster liquor. Put the oysters, oyster liquor, butter and salt back in the large stock pot. Simmer until the edges of the oysters begin to curl.

While waiting for the oysters to curl, scald the milk in a saucepan. Add the scalded milk to the oysters once they have curled; serve immediately. Serves 4.

Garnish with parsley and serve with French bread.

FRIED OYSTERS.

1 dozen oysters, steamed and dried	1/8 tsp. freshly ground pepper
2 eggs, beaten	1 c. flour
1 tsp. salt	3/4 c. milk

Beat eggs in a small mixing bowl; add salt and pepper. Combine the flour and milk in a medium size bowl; stir until blended. Add the eggs to the flour and milk, and mix until you have a smooth batter.

Dip the oysters, one at a time, in the batter. Gently place the oysters into hot oil. Fry until golden; remove and drain on a paper towel. Serve with lemon wedges. Serves 2.

LAMB CHOPS, BREADED.

4 lamb chops	1 c. dry bread crumbs
1/2 tsp. salt	2 eggs, beaten
1/4 tsp. freshly ground pepper	shortening or oil for frying

Wash and pat dry the chops. Sprinkle both sides with salt and pepper. Dredge the chops through the bread crumbs, into the eggs, and then back through the bread crumbs. Fry in 1/2" of hot shortening or oil, until golden brown on both sides; about 20 minutes. Pierce with a fork to see if the juices run clear. Serve with baked macaroni & cheese and sugar peas.

OYSTER PATTIES.

1 lb. oysters, chopped	2 T. lemon juice
(steamed or canned)	1/4 tsp. salt
2 c. soft bread crumbs	dash freshly ground pepper
1/3 c. onion, chopped	2 T. parsley, chopped
1/4 c. milk	1/2 c. dry bread crumbs
2 eggs, slightly beaten	3 T. butter or margarine

In a bowl, combine the first nine ingredients; mix thoroughly. Shape into eight patties, about 3/4" thick. Place the dry bread crumbs in a shallow dish. Next, press the patties into the bread crumbs, being sure to coast them evenly on both sides.

Melt the butter or margarine over medium high heat in a large frying pan. Cook patties on both sides until golden. Place patties on a paper towel to drain off excess oil. Remove to a platter and serve immediately. Serves 4.

Note: If you don't like oysters try substituting clams.

MISSISSIPPI CORNBREAD.

1 c. corn meal	2 1/2 tsp. baking powder
1 c. flour	2 T. shortening
1 tsp. salt	2 eggs, beaten
2 T. sugar	2 c. buttermilk

In a large bowl, blend the dry ingredients; cut in shortening until the mixture is crumbly. Add the eggs and milk, stirring until combined. Do not over beat batter.

Pour the batter into a greased loaf pan. Bake at 400° for 20-25 minutes, or until a toothpick inserted comes out clean. Allow to stand in pan for 5 minutes, then place on board and cut into slices. This goes great with chicken gumbo soup.

Note: If you do not have buttermilk, add 1 tsp. vinegar to 1 cup of milk and let stand for 5 minutes.

OMELET.

This is a basic omelet recipe, but it can be used for the basis of many delicious recipes. Try filling it with cheese, ham, bacon, peppers, onions, mushrooms, or anything else you'd like to experiment with.

3 eggs	1 tsp. water
1/4 tsp. salt	1 T. butter
1/8 tsp. freshly ground pepper	

Beat the eggs, salt, pepper and water in a medium bowl, until the eggs are frothy. Melt the butter in an omelet pan or non-stick skillet, over medium high heat. Once the butter begins to bubble, add the eggs. Let the eggs cook untouched, for 1 minute. Using a spatula, gently draw the edges of the omelet to the center, while tipping the pan on an angle. This will allow the uncooked center to run to the outside; do this in several places. Cover the pan and allow the omelet to cook for 2-3 minutes, or until the center is firm. Fold in half and serve.

CORN BATTER CAKES.

2 1/4 c. flour	1/3 c. sugar
1/2 c. corn meal	1 1/2 c. water
1 1/4 tsp. baking powder	1 c. milk
1 tsp. salt	1 egg, beaten
2 T. butter, melted	

In a medium sauce pan, bring the water to a boil; add the corn meal and boil for 5 minutes. In a large bowl, combine the dry ingredients, mix well. Next, add the corn meal mixture, milk, egg and butter. Stir to combine, being sure not to over mix the batter.

Cook on a griddle or in a frying pan, as you would pancakes. Serve warm, with butter and jelly, or your favorite syrup. Makes about 12. Garnish with orange slices.

BUCKWHEAT CAKES.

Whenever I think of these pancakes, I remember my childhood days when my family visited my parents' hometown in upstate New York. Before we came home, we had to visit the grocery store to bring back some buckwheat pancake mix. This recipe is from my Grandmother, Anna Louise Teeter. She taught her daughters how to make them, and my Aunt Merty shared it with me, and granted me permission to share it with you.

1 1/2 c. buckwheat flour	1 1/2 c. buttermilk
1 c. white flour	1/2 c. hot water
1 tsp. salt	1/4 c. boiling water
1 tsp. baking soda	

In a large bowl, combine the flours and salt together. Add the buttermilk and 1/2 cup of the hot water. Mix well and cover. Allow this mixture to sit overnight in a warm place. The next morning, combine the 1/2 cup of boiling water and baking soda in a small bowl. When it bubbles, add it to the buckwheat mixture and stir to blend.

Cook on a hot griddle or frying pan, just as you would for pancakes. Serve immediately with butter and syrup. Makes about 12-15.

Note: If you don't have buttermilk you can substitute by adding 1 tsp. vinegar to a cup of milk. Let stand for 5 minutes, stir and use.

VEAL CUTLETS, BREADED.

If you prefer not to use veal, try using pork, chicken or even venison.

1 lb. veal cutlets, 1/8" thick	1 c. dry bread crumbs
1/2 tsp. salt	3 T. butter
1/4 tsp. freshly ground pepper	3 T. oil
1/3 c. flour	1 lemon, sliced thin
4 eggs, lightly beaten	

Coat the cutlets with the salt and pepper; let stand for 10 minutes. Place the flour, eggs, and bread crumbs in separate bowls or pie plates.

Heat the butter and oil in a large skillet over medium high heat. Dredge the veal in the flour first, then the eggs, and finally, the bread crumbs. Gently place them in the skillet and cook until they have browned. If you cannot cook the cutlets all at once, place the cooked ones in a covered dish and place in a 250° oven while you cook the rest. Serve on a platter garnished with lemon slices.

VEAL CUTLETS, PLAIN.

If you prefer not to use veal, try using pork, chicken or even venison.

1 lb. veal cutlets, 1" thick	1/8 tsp. freshly ground pepper
1 T. butter	1/2 c. dry white wine
1/2 T. oil	1/2 tsp. thyme
1/4 tsp. salt	1 T. butter, cut into pieces

Wash and dry the cutlets. Melt 2 tablespoons of butter and the oil, in a large frying pan. Cook the cutlets over medium high heat for 5-6 minutes on each side. Remove the cutlets and place on a serving platter. Deglaze the pan with the wine. Add the thyme and cook for 5 minutes to reduce. Remove from the heat and stir in the butter pieces. Pour around the veal cutlets and serve.

LIVER AND BACON.

This is not one of my favorites, in fact, I don't eat it. That's why I had to get my best friend to test the recipe on her husband. Thankfully, it is one of his favorites!

1 1/2 lb. calf's liver	1/8 tsp. freshly ground pepper
1/2" thick	3/4 c. flour
1/2 lb. bacon strips	1 tsp. salt

Place the liver in a shallow pan and add enough boiling water to cover it. Allow this to stand for 5 minutes. Meanwhile, fry the bacon in a large sauté pan over medium heat until done. Remove and drain on a towel. Set the pan with the bacon fat aside.

Drain the liver and pat it dry. Cut it into serving pieces and sprinkle with salt and pepper. Heat the bacon fat over medium high heat and add the liver pieces. Cook until well browned on all sides, about 8-10 minutes. Remove the liver, place on a serving dish and garnish with the bacon strips.

CITY ITEMS

Midnight Lunches

At the solicitation of its many guests, Mons. Prodsosaltia & Riche will hereafter keep the Maison Doree open until 1 a. m. Finest imported and game lunches a specialty, and choice Eastern oysters at fifty cents per plate. Coffee, bread and cold meat or ham, 25 cents.

Advertisement for the Maison Doree

Tombstone Epitaph, 1882

ROAST QUAIL.

6 quail	salt and pepper
6 large oysters	1 c. flour
6 bacon slices	butter or margarine, softened

Wash the quail, inside and out; pat dry. Place one oyster in the cavity of each bird. Close the bird by tying the legs together.

Combine flour, salt and pepper in a shallow pan. Dredge the birds in the flour to coat evenly. Butter the breasts of the bird and lay a half slice of bacon over each leg. Place in a roasting pan and bake at 350°, uncovered, for 25 minutes or until done. Remove bacon before slicing.

Note: If you can't get quail in your area, substitute capons or Cornish game hens.

VENISON STEAK WITH JELLY.

Even though venison is not very popular today, it can be found in some stores. Hunting for venison is an old tradition that came from living off the land. My father still hunts for venison and keeps this family tradition alive. For as long as I can remember, we always had venison for dinner. Although I must admit that as a child, I cringed at the thought of venison for dinner! I remember my mother trying to trick my sister and me by saying it wasn't really venison, but we usually knew.

4 venison steaks, 1/2" thick juice of 1 lemon
1/2 c. oil currant jelly

Marinate venison in oil and lemon juice for 2 hours. (If the venison is wild and not farm-raised, you may want to soak it overnight in salted water before marinating it in the oil and lemon. This will remove some of the wild flavor.) Broil or grill the steaks for 7 to 10 minutes or until desired doneness is reached. Place on a serving platter and serve with currant jelly.

CURRANT JELLY

2 c. currants sugar

Wash and drain the currants, but do not remove the stems. Put them in a large saucepan that has been placed over medium high heat. Start crushing the currants with a masher while they are heating. Once you have crushed all the currants and they have cooked down, strain through cheesecloth. Measure the strained juice, and measure out equal amounts of sugar. Place the juice and sugar in the saucepan and cook over medium high heat until it begins to boil. Boil rapidly until the jelly begins to thicken. Take a spoon and coat it with the jelly, if 2-3 drops run to the end of the spoon and then hang on for a second or two, the jelly is done. Place in containers, and keep refrigerated until ready to use. Makes 2 pints.

weapon, concealed or otherwise (except
the same be carried openly in sight and in
the hand), within the limits of the City of
Tombstone.   JOHN CARR, Mayor.

RUSS HOUSE.

SUNDAY BILL OF FARE.

Dinner.

SOUP.

Consomme and Chicken.

BOILED.

Corned Beef; Ham, au Champagne Sauce;
Mutton, Caper Sauce.

ENTREES.

Roast Duck; Tongue, German Sauce;
Lamb Saute, with Green Peas;
Roast Venison, Apple Sauce;
Veal Cutlets, Mushroom Sauce.

ROASTS.

Short Ribs of Beef, Mutton, Lamb, Pork,
Veal.

VEGETABLES.

Corn, Beans, Potatoes. Assorted.

PASTRY.

Assorted Pies and Jelly Cake.

PUDDING.

Green Apple Dumplings, Brandy Sauce.

DESSERT.

Oranges and Apples.

Tea and Coffee or Wine.   Wines to order.

Russ House Bill of Fare   *Tombstone Epitaph, 1882*

VENISON CUTLETS WITH APPLES.

4 apples
1 T. powdered sugar
1/3 c. port wine
2 tsp. butter or margarine
12 candied cherries, halved

6 venison cutlets, 1/2" thick
salt and pepper
3 T. butter or margarine
3 T. butter

Put the apples in a dish; sprinkle with powdered sugar and then cover with the wine; soak for 30 minutes. Drain, reserving the wine and juices. Sauté the apples in 2 teaspoons of butter until tender; set aside.

Rub the cutlets with salt and pepper. Melt one tablespoon of butter in a frying pan, add the cutlets and sauté over medium high heat for 3-4 minutes. Set aside and cover. Add the remaining three tablespoons of butter to the pan and melt. Pour in the reserved wine and juice; add the cherries. Once this has heated through, reheat the cutlets in the wine sauce. Arrange the cutlets on a serving platter, pour the wine sauce over them and garnish with the sautéed apples.

Note: If your venison is not farm raised, it may need to be soaked overnight in salt water to help remove some the "wild" flavor. To do this, place the meat in a glass or plastic dish and add enough water to cover the meat. Add 1 tsp. salt for each quart of water. Refrigerate and soak overnight. Rinse and it's ready to be cooked.

CREAM PIE #2.

CAKE RECIPE

1 c. butter, room temperature	1 c. milk
1 1/2 c. sugar	3 1/2 c. flour
4 eggs, beaten	5 tsp. baking powder

CREAM FILLING

3/4 c. sugar	2 c. milk, scalded
1/8 tsp. salt	1/2 tsp. lemon extract
1/3 c. flour	1 tsp. vanilla extract
2 eggs, slightly beaten	

In a large bowl, cream butter; gradually add the sugar, mix well. Add the beaten eggs and combine. Set aside. In a small bowl, sift flour and baking powder; gradually add the flour mixture, alternating with the milk into the butter and egg batter. Beat well until combined.

Grease and flour two or three (depending on how thick you want the layers) round cake pans. Take a piece of parchment or wax paper and line the bottoms of the cake pans. Pour the batter in the pans and bake at 350° for 30 minutes or until done. Cool in pans for 10 minutes; cool completely before filling. While the cake is cooling make the cream filling.

In a large saucepan, scald the milk. In a separate bowl, combine the dry ingredients, blend well. Gradually add the eggs, mix until combined. Slowly add this mixture to the scalded milk. Cook in a double boiler until thick; stirring constantly for about 5 minutes. Cool. Add the lemon and vanilla. Once the cake and filling have cooled completely, spread the filling between the layers. Dust the cake with powdered sugar.

Note: If you do not have a double boiler, a metal bowl over a saucepan of gently boiling water may be substituted.

GREEN APPLE DUMPLINGS, BRANDY SAUCE.

Don't let the name "green apple" throw you off. Remember, back then, green referred to fruit that was fresh and not dried. I made these for my family last Christmas and they were a huge success!

6 large apples, peeled & cored	3/4 tsp. cinnamon
1 T. lemon juice	1 tsp. grated lemon rind
1/4 tsp. salt	1 double pie crust
4 T. butter	

Brush the apples with the lemon juice to prevent them from turning brown. Combine the remaining ingredients, except the pie crust, and blend well.

Roll the dough on a floured surface to 1/8" thick. Cut into squares, large enough to cover the apples. Place the apples on the squares and fill the centers with the brown sugar filling. Bring the corners of the dough up to the center and pinch the seams closed.

Bake on a greased baking sheet for 25-30 minutes at 350°, or until the apples are tender.

BRANDY SAUCE

1/2 c. butter	2 T. hot water
1 c. powdered sugar	2 T. brandy
1 egg, beaten	

Beat the butter and sugar together in a sauce pan until light and fluffy, over medium heat. Stir in the egg and water, and continue stirring while the sauce starts to thicken. Add the brandy and cook for 1 minute.

express. Don't Send by Registered Letter or Post Office Order. Orders of $5.00
and upwards by express can be sent at our ex-
pense. Special rates for clubs of $10.00 and up-
wards. All communicated to a connected with the
Denver City Lottery, and orders for tickets should
be addressed to   G. N. DeGROIO.
Box 2077.   J3 3t   Denver, Colo.

BOSS DINNER

AT THE

Boss Restaurant.

Bill of Fare for Sunday Dinner.

SOUP.
Oyster Soup and Chicken Broth.

ROASTS.
Roast Beef. Roast Pork and Apple Sauce. Lamb
and Green Peas. Chicken Roast
and Fricasseed,

VEGETABLES.
Cabbage. Turnips. Green Corn. Tomatoe and
Potatoes.

DESSERT.
English Plum Pudding   Ice Cocoanut Cake.
Jelly Rolls   Marble Cake. Raisin,
Custard and Green Peach Pie.

BEVERAGES.
Tea. Coffee. Claret Wine.

Mrs. Jeanie Harding. Proprietress.
Allen Street, between Sixth and Seventh.
                    J11 1t

Solomon Lodge. U. D. F. & A. M.,
The officers and members of the above named
lodge are hereby notified to attend a special meet-
ing this, Saturday, evening at 7:30 o'clock, for
work in the first degree. All sojourning brethren

Boss Restaurant Bill of Fare   Tombstone Epitaph, 1882

ROAST BEEF.

4-6 lb. eye round roast	1/2 c. flour
6 bacon strips	2 T. salt

Preheat the oven to 450°. Rinse roast and pat dry. Rub the salt on all sides of the roast. Dredge the salted roast in the flour. Next, wrap the roast with the bacon strips.

Place on a baking rack, which has been placed in a roasting pan. Cook the meat, uncovered, at 450° for 15 minutes. Reduce the heat to 325° and cook for an hour for a medium roast. Remember that even after you take the roast from the oven it will continue to cook for a few more minutes.

Remove the roast and allow it to sit for 10 minutes before carving. Place the carved meat in a covered dish until you are ready to serve it.

After removing the roast from the pan, skim off any excess fat from the pan juices. Add 1 1/2 cups of boiling water to the pan and scrape the bottom to remove the crusty bits.

Arrange the meat on a serving platter, and pour the gravy over the meat slices. Garnish with fresh parsley or thyme. Serves 4. Mashed potatoes and string beans go well with this roast.

CABBAGE.

1 head cabbage	3 tsp. butter or margarine
1/4 tsp. baking soda	salt & pepper to taste
1/2 tsp. salt	

Wash the cabbage and remove the outside leaves. Cut into quarters and remove the white stalk.

Place the cabbage, baking soda and salt in a large stockpot and cover with cold water. Bring this to a boil over high heat and cook uncovered for 40-50 minutes or until desired tenderness. Drain the cabbage; add the butter and salt and pepper to taste. Garnish with dill weed. Makes about 6 servings.

TURNIPS.

Turnips have always been a traditional holiday favorite in my family and my husband's as well. They're really delicious, which is why I don't know why we only eat them around the holidays. We should be enjoying them all year long.

3 medium turnips	4 T. butter or margarine
1/2 tsp. salt	salt & pepper to taste

Peel the turnips and cut into cubes. Place the cubed turnips in a medium pot and cover with cold water. Bring this to a boil and continue cooking for about 25 minutes, or until tender. Drain the turnips and mash. Add the butter and salt and pepper to taste. Garnish with parsley sprig.

Note: If you can't get turnips, try substituting rutabagas instead. They're delicious, too.

RAISIN PIE.

I had never heard of raisin pie until my father-in-law told me that his Aunt Bertha used to make it for him. As they used to say in Tombstone, "give it a trial."

1/3 c. lemon juice	2 c. raisins
1 tsp. grated lemon peel	1 1/4 c. water
1/2 c. orange juice	6 T. flour
2 tsp. grated orange peel	1/2 c. brandy
1 c. brown sugar	1 double crust pie*, unbaked

Combine the first six ingredients and 1 1/4 cups of water; bring to a boil. In a small bowl, combine the flour and brandy; the mixture should resemble a smooth paste. Gradually add this to the raisin mixture, stirring constantly. Cook over high heat for 5 minutes.

Pour into a 9-inch pie pan, cover with crust and flute edges. Bake at 400° for 40 minutes.

*See recipe on page 146.

ICE COCONUT CAKE.

2/3 c. shortening
1 3/4 c. sugar
3 c. flour
3 tsp. baking powder
1/2 tsp. salt

1 c. milk
1 tsp. lemon extract
4 eggs
1 c. coconut

In a large bowl, cream shortening and sugar; beat until light and fluffy. In a small bowl, sift the dry ingredients together. Alternating with the milk, eggs and lemon, gradually add the flour mixture to the butter and sugar. Beat on high for 2 minutes.

Pour the batter into three 9-inch cake pans that have been greased and floured. Bake at 350° for 25 minutes. Remove from the oven and allow the cake to cool in the pan for 10 minutes. Turn the cake layers out onto cake racks to cool completely.

Place coconut and whipped cream between cake layers. Spread whipped cream on top and sides, and sprinkle with coconut.

Refrigerate for a minimum of 20 minutes. Garnish with a mint leaf or fresh berries.

WHIPPED CREAM

2 pt. heavy cream
1 tsp. vanilla

4 T. sugar

Combine the above in a chilled bowl; whip until fluffy.

MARBLE CAKE.

2/3 c. butter, room temp.	4 tsp. baking powder
1 3/4 c. sugar	1 tsp. salt
4 eggs, beaten	1 c. milk
1 tsp. vanilla	2 oz. (square) chocolate,
3 1/3 c. cake flour	melted

In a large bowl, cream the butter and sugar together until well combined. Add eggs and vanilla, mix well. In a separate bowl, sift the dry ingredients together. Gradually add the dry ingredients to the egg mixture, alternating with the milk. Beat until smooth. Place 1/3 of the batter in a separate bowl and add the melted chocolate, stir to combine. Grease and flour a 10-inch tube pan. Drop the batter into the pan by spoonfuls, alternating the vanilla and chocolate batters. Bake at 350° for 1 hour or until done. Test for doneness by inserting a toothpick into the cake; if it comes out clean, the cake is done. Allow the cake to cool in the pan for 15 minutes. Turn onto a cake rack and cool completely before frosting.

CHOCOLATE FUDGE ICING

2 oz. chocolate	3 c. powdered sugar
3 T. butter or margarine	1 tsp. vanilla
1/4 c. milk	

In a large saucepan, combine the first three ingredients. Cook over low heat until the chocolate has melted. Stir in the sugar and vanilla; cook over medium heat for 3-5 minutes until the mixture bubbles. Remove from the heat, strain, and immediately pour over the cake. Allow to harden and serve.

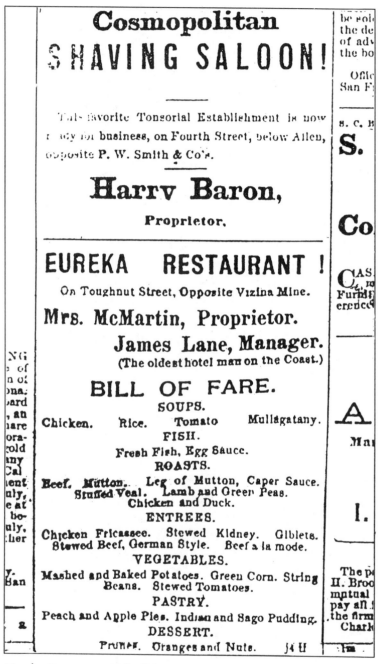

Eureka Restaurant Bill of Fare

Tombstone Epitaph, 1882

TOMATO SOUP.

2 T. butter or margarine
1 turnip, sliced
1 onion, sliced
1 carrot, sliced
1 stalk celery, sliced
4 T. flour
4 c. beef broth

1 28 oz. can tomatoes
   or 3 c. fresh, chopped
1 bay leaf
1 pinch grated nutmeg
1/2 tsp. salt
1/8 tsp. freshly ground pepper

In a large pot, melt the butter and cook the carrot, turnip, onion, and celery over medium high heat. Once the mixture is golden in color, add the flour. Cook for an additional 2 minutes. Add the remaining ingredients, bring to a boil. Reduce the heat to low and cook until all the vegetables are tender. Force the mixture through a sieve, or puree and strain. Season to taste with salt and pepper.

Place back on the stove, bring to a boil. Serve warm with croutons.

Note: To reduce the acidity in this recipe, dissolve 1 tsp. baking soda in 2 T. water. Pour this in the soup after you have reduced the heat.

MULLIGATAWNY.

1/4 c. butter or margarine
1 c. chicken, diced
1/4 c. onion, chopped
1/4 c. carrot, chopped
1/4 c. celery, chopped
1 green pepper, diced
1 apple, diced
1/4 c. flour

1/2 tsp. mace
2 cloves
sprig of parsley
1 tsp. curry powder
1/2 tsp. salt
1/8 tsp. freshly ground pepper
1 c. tomatoes, diced
4 c. chicken stock

In a large pot melt the butter, cook the chicken and vegetables over medium high heat until lightly brown. Add the flour and spices; stir well. Next add the tomatoes and chicken stock; simmer for 40 minutes. Taste for seasoning and adjust with salt and pepper. Serve with steamed rice.

ROAST DUCK.

1 5 lb. duck
2 apples, cored & quartered
1/4 c. raisins
1/4 c. orange flavored liqueur

2 garlic cloves, crushed
1 tsp. salt
1/2 tsp. freshly ground pepper
1 c. orange juice

Place the raisins and liqueur in a small bowl and allow to soak for 15 minutes. Meanwhile, wash and clean the duck; pat dry. Drain the raisins and add the liqueur to the orange juice. Add the apples to the raisins and mix well; stuff this into the duck. Rub the duck with the garlic, salt and pepper.

Place in an uncovered roasting pan and cook at 325° for 2 to 2 1/2 hours or until desired doneness is reached. Baste the duck about every 15 minutes with the orange juice mixture. Slice and serve with currant or cranberry jelly.

STEWED BEEF, GERMAN STYLE.

5 T. oil
3 lb. beef chuck, cubed
5 large onions, chopped
3 garlic cloves, crushed
2 T. caraway seeds
1 T. marjoram
3 T. flour

2 tsp. salt
1/2 tsp. freshly ground pepper
3 c. hot water
1 c. beer
1 c. tomato puree
8 mushrooms, sliced

Heat 3 tablespoons of the oil in a large stock pot over high heat. When the oil is hot, add the cubed beef and brown on all sides. Transfer the meat to a plate or bowl.

Sauté the onions, garlic, caraway seeds, and marjoram in the remaining 3 tablespoons of oil over medium heat. Cook for about 10 minutes, or until the onions have turned golden. Add the cooked beef back to the pot. Sprinkle with flour, salt and pepper. Stir well to incorporate the flour, and cook for about 3 minutes. Add the water and beer; bring to a boil. Reduce the heat, cover and simmer for one hour. Stir in the tomato puree and cook for another 1 1/4 hours. Next, add the mushrooms and allow to cook uncovered, for 45 minutes. Serve with crusty bread.

PEACH PIE.

1/2 c. light brown sugar
1/4 tsp. salt
2 T. flour
1/2 c. honey

6 large peaches, peeled
& sliced, 1/8"
2 T. butter, cut up
1 double pie crust*, unbaked

Combine the brown sugar, salt, and flour in a large bowl. Stir in the honey and mix well. Add the peaches and toss to coat evenly. Pour into a 9" pie pan, dot the pie with the butter bits, and cover with the second crust. Make 3 or 4 slits in the top of the pie and bake at 450° for 15 minutes. Reduce the heat to 350° and bake an additional 35 minutes, or until the peaches are tender. If the pie crust edges begin the brown too much, cover with aluminum foil. Allow to cool for 30 minutes before cutting. Serve with whipped cream or vanilla ice cream.

*See recipe on page 146.

INDIAN PUDDING.

3/4 c. corn meal
4 c. milk, scalded
1 tsp. salt

1/2 c. molasses
1/3 c. sugar
5 tsp. butter

Place corn meal in a large double boiler or metal bowl over simmering water; slowly pour the milk over the corn meal. Stir to combine and allow to cook for 20 minutes. Add the sugar, salt, and molasses, stir.

Pour into a buttered baking dish and bake at 275° for 2 hours; remove from the oven and beat the pudding with a whisk to combine. Return the pudding to the oven and bake an additional hour. The pudding may also be poured into 6 small ramekins and baked for about the same time. Serve warm.

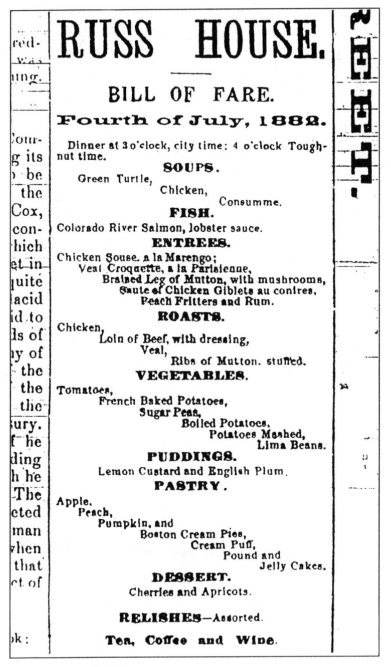

RUSS HOUSE.

BILL OF FARE.

Fourth of July, 1882.

Dinner at 3 o'clock, city time; 4 o'clock Tough-nut time.

SOUPS.

Green Turtle,
Chicken,
Consumme.

FISH.

Colorado River Salmon, lobster sauce.

ENTREES.

Chicken Souse. a la Marengo;
Veal Croquette, a la Parisienne,
Braised Leg of Mutton, with mushrooms,
Saute of Chicken Giblets au conires,
Peach Fritters and Rum.

ROASTS.

Chicken,
Loin of Beef, with dressing,
Veal,
Ribs of Mutton. stuffed.

VEGETABLES.

Tomatoes,
French Baked Potatoes,
Sugar Peas,
Boiled Potatoes,
Potatoes Mashed,
Lima Beans.

PUDDINGS.

Lemon Custard and English Plum.

PASTRY.

Apple,
Peach,
Pumpkin, and
Boston Cream Pies,
Cream Puff,
Pound and
Jelly Cakes.

DESSERT.

Cherries and Apricots.

RELISHES—Assorted.

Tea, Coffee and Wine.

Russ House Bill of Fare   *Tombstone Epitaph, 1882*

VEAL CROQUETTES, A LA PARISIENNE.

The cooks of the 1880's were often frugal in their choices. Croquettes, for example, were an excellent way for them to use leftover meat from a previous meal.

2 c. veal, cooked* & chopped	1 egg yolk
1/2 tsp. salt	1 c. white sauce**
1/8 tsp. freshly ground pepper	bread crumbs
1/8 tsp. onion powder	oil for frying

Mix the veal, salt, pepper and onion powder together in a bowl, stir well. Slowly add half of the white sauce. Mix together. Continue adding the white sauce, but be sure not to add too much, as you want to be able to shape the mixture. Form the mixture into desired shapes, such as cones, balls, cylinders, etc. Roll the shapes in the bread crumbs first, then in the eggs, and then back in the bread crumbs.

Gently place the croquettes in the hot oil and cook until they are golden brown. Drain on a towel. Arrange croquettes on a serving platter and pour the Parisienne sauce around them.

A LA PARISIENNE

2 c. white sauce**	1/2 tsp. salt
2 egg yolks	1/4 tsp. white pepper
1/2 c. heavy cream	1 tsp. lemon juice

Heat the white sauce in a large sauce pan over medium heat. Beat the egg yolks and cream in a small bowl. Gradually add a 1/2 cup of the white sauce to the eggs, stirring quickly. Now add the eggs to the sauce pan and stir constantly. Allow to come to a boil and cook one minute from the boiling point. Stir in salt, pepper, and lemon juice.

See recipe on page 185 if you do not have any leftover veal.
**See recipe on page 132.*

PEACH FRITTERS, RUM SAUCE.

3/4 c. Rum	2 T. sugar
1 1/3 c. flour, sifted	1 egg
1/4 tsp. salt	2/3 c. milk
2 tsp. baking powder	4 peaches
shortening for frying	

Pit and peel the peaches. Slice them about 1/8" thickness and place in a shallow container. Pour the brandy or rum over the peaches and set aside for at least one half hour. In a medium size bowl, sift dry ingredients together. Add the egg and milk; blend well. The batter should be thick enough to coat the peach slices. Adjust the thickness of the batter with additional milk. In a frying pan, over medium high heat, heat enough shortening to come up 2 inches in the pan. While the shortening is heating up, drain the peaches (reserve 2 T. of the rum for the sauce) and pat dry. Once the oil gets hot enough, dip the peaches into the batter. Drop gently into the oil and fry 2-3 minutes or until golden. Remove from the oil and drain on a paper towel. Arrange on a serving platter, dust with confectioner's sugar and serve with Rum sauce.

RUM SAUCE

1/2 c. butter	2 T. hot water
1 c. powdered sugar	2 T. rum
1 egg, beaten	

Beat the butter and sugar together in a sauce pan until light and fluffy, over medium heat. Stir in the egg and water, and continue stirring while the sauce starts to thicken. Add the rum and cook for 1 minute.

LOIN OF BEEF WITH DRESSING.

4 lb. filet of beef or
beef tenderloin
2 T. butter
1 T. onion, chopped
1/2 c. celery, diced
1/2 c. carrot, diced
1 tsp. salt

1/4 tsp. freshly ground pepper
1 c. fresh bread crumbs
1 T. oil
1 T. butter
2 c. brown stock*
1 T. cornstarch
2 T. red wine

Make a horizontal slit, 1" wide through the center of the filet. In a medium skillet, sauté the onion, celery, carrot, salt and pepper in 2 T. butter for 10 minutes. Place the vegetables in a medium bowl and add the bread crumbs; stir to combine.

Stuff the filet with the vegetable dressing you just made, leaving a 1/2" space on both ends. In a large ovenproof pan, melt the butter and oil over medium high heat. Sear the stuffed filet on all sides. Remove the filet from the pan and set aside; drain the butter and oil from the pan. Return the filet to the pan and add the stock. Place in a 350° oven and cook, uncovered, for 50-55 minutes. The meat thermometer should register 140° for a medium rare roast.

When done, remove the roast from the pan and allow to sit 10 minutes before carving. Meanwhile, dissolve the cornstarch in the wine. Place the roasting pan over medium heat and bring the pan juices to a boil. Whisking constantly, add the thickened wine and cook until the desired consistency is achieved. Carve the meat and serve with the gravy.

See recipe on page 136.

LIMA BEANS.

4 c. fresh lima beans
4 c. water
1 tsp. salt

1/4 tsp. freshly ground pepper
1 T. butter

Boil the water in a medium dutch oven; add the salt and lima beans. Reduce the heat to medium and cook for 25-30 minutes, or until the beans become tender. Drain and toss with butter.

LEMON CUSTARD PUDDING.

4 egg yolks
1 c. sugar
1 T. cornstarch
2/3 c. water

grating of 1 lemon
juice of 1 lemon
4 eggs white
3 T. sugar

Combine the above ingredients in a large bowl and mix well. Pour into a large oven proof casserole or individual custard cups and bake at 325° for 30 minutes. While this is baking, stiffly beat the egg whites in a bowl. Gradually add the 3 T. sugar. After the custard is cooked, spread the whites on top and out back in the over until the top is golden. A knife inserted will come out clean when done.

BOSTON CREAM PIE.

Even though we think of Boston Cream Pie as having a chocolate topping, many of the older recipes do not call for it. Therefore, I have chosen to give you a recipe that more closely resembles what was used in Tombstone.

2 c. sifted flour	2 eggs, beaten
2 1/2 tsp. baking powder	1/2 c. milk
1/2 tsp. salt	1 tsp. vanilla
1/2 c. butter, softened	cream filling
2/3 c. sugar	powdered sugar for dusting

Sift the flour, baking powder, and salt together in a small bowl; set aside. Combine the butter and sugar in a large bowl, and beat until light and fluffy. Add the eggs and mix well. Add the sifted flour to the creamed butter, alternating with the milk. Mix until well combined and light. Add the vanilla and stir to combine.

Grease and flour two 9" cake pans; line with wax paper. Pour the batter into the pans and cake at 375° for 25 minutes. Test with a toothpick. Cool the cakes in the pans for 10 minutes. Complete the cooling by removing the cakes from the pans and the wax paper; set on cake racks. When completely cooled, fill with cream filling and dust with powdered sugar.

CREAM FILLING

1 3/4 c. milk, scalded	2 eggs, beaten
3/4 c. sugar	1 T. butter
1/4 c. flour	1 tsp. vanilla
1/4 tsp. salt	

Scald the milk in a large saucepan. Meanwhile, combine the sugar, flour, and salt in a small bowl. Once the milk has been scalded, add the flour mixture. Cook over medium heat and stir constantly until mixture has thickened, about 5 minutes. Beat the eggs in a small bowl. Slowly add a 1/2 cup of the cooked mixture, stirring constantly. Once this is done, add the eggs to the saucepan and stir continuously for 2 minutes. Add the butter and vanilla; mix well. Remove from the heat and cool.

CREAM PUFFS.

1/2 c. shortening
1/2 tsp. salt
1 c. water, boiling

1 c. flour
4 eggs

Place the shortening, salt and water in a large saucepan. Bring to a boil over high heat. Once it begins to boil, reduce the heat to low and add the flour. Stir vigorously until the dough forms a ball and clings to the spoon. Remove from the heat and add 1 egg at a time. After each addition, beat thoroughly. After the last eggs has been added, continue beating until the dough becomes thick and shiny. Place 1 tablespoon, two inches apart, on an ungreased baking sheet. Bake at 450° for 20 minutes, then reduce the heat to 350° and bake an additional 20 minutes. Cool. Remove the tops and fill with cream filling*. Place tops back on, and dust with powdered sugar.

*See recipe on page 208or 191.

Note: These do not sit well for very long, and should be eaten shortly after preparing them.

POUND CAKE.

1/2 c. butter, softened
1 c. sugar
5 eggs
2 T. brandy

1/2 tsp. freshly grated nutmeg
1 tsp. baking soda
1/2 c. milk
2 c. flour

Beat the butter until light and fluffy, about 7 minutes. Add the sugar, eggs and brandy; beat for another 5 minutes.

In a separate bowl, sift the flour, nutmeg and baking soda. Alternating with the milk, add the sifted flour to the butter and sugar. Mix on high for 5 minutes. You want this batter to be light and fluffy. Place in a greased loaf pan, and bake at 325° for 1 hour, or until done.

Cool in pan for 10 minutes and remove. Allow to cool completely on a wire rack. Slice and serve with ice cream or fresh fruit.

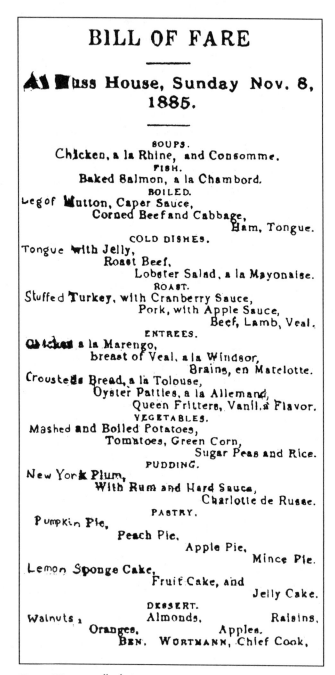

BILL OF FARE

At Russ House, Sunday Nov. 8, 1885.

SOUPS.
Chicken, a la Rhine, and Consomme.
FISH.
Baked Salmon, a la Chambord.
BOILED.
Leg of Mutton, Caper Sauce,
Corned Beef and Cabbage,
Ham, Tongue.
COLD DISHES.
Tongue with Jelly,
Roast Beef,
Lobster Salad, a la Mayonaise.
ROAST.
Stuffed Turkey, with Cranberry Sauce,
Pork, with Apple Sauce,
Beef, Lamb, Veal.
ENTREES.
Chicken a la Marengo,
breast of Veal, a la Windsor,
Brains, en Matelotte.
Croustells Bread, a la Tolouse,
Oyster Patties, a la Allemand,
Queen Fritters, Vanil, a Flavor.
VEGETABLES.
Mashed and Boiled Potatoes,
Tomatoes, Green Corn,
Sugar Peas and Rice.
PUDDING.
New York Plum,
With Rum and Hard Sauce,
Charlotte de Russe.
PASTRY.
Pumpkin Pie,
Peach Pie,
Apple Pie,
Mince Pie.
Lemon Sponge Cake,
Fruit Cake, and
Jelly Cake.
DESSERT.
Walnuts, Almonds, Raisins,
Oranges, Apples.
BEN. WORTMANN, Chief Cook,

Russ House Bill of Fare   *Daily Record Epitaph, 1885*

STUFFED TURKEY.

16-20 lb. turkey   2 T. butter or margarine,
                                                     softened

Preheat oven to 350°. Remove excess fat from the cavity of
the bird; discard. Set the giblets, neck, heart and liver aside. Rinse
and dry the turkey, inside and out. Stuff the cavity and the neck
area with the recipe below. Once stuffed, truss the neck area, then
the cavity. Before cutting your string, be sure to wrap the legs as
well.

Rub the butter or margarine all over the bird. Place the turkey
in a large covered roasting pan. Be sure to baste the bird every
30-40 minutes, until done. To obtain a golden color, remove the
lid 30 minutes before cooking time is up. A bird this size should
take approximately 3 1/2 to 4 hours to cook. You can stick a
fork in the inside leg area to see if the juices run clear; once they
do, the turkey is done.

STUFFING

1 lb. fresh sausage meat   2 large eggs, beaten lightly
1 c. onions, minced   1 small garlic clove, minced
turkey liver, minced (optional)   1/2 tsp. thyme
1 lb. fresh mushrooms, diced   1/2 bay leaf, pulverized
2 T. capers, minced   4 c. homemade croutons
salt & pepper to taste

Sauté sausage until no longer pink. Drain, reserving drippings.
Place sausage in a large bowl. Place 2 T. drippings in large frying
pan and sauté onions over medium heat, for 7 minutes or until
tender. Add liver and sauté for an additional minute or until liver
is firm. Place the liver and onions in the bowl with the sausage.
Sauté mushrooms and capers in 1 T. additional drippings until
tender, about 3 to 4 minutes. Add to bowl with sausage. Mix in
the remaining ingredients, blend well. Allow to cool and then
stuff the turkey. Makes enough for a 16-20 lb. turkey.

CRANBERRY SAUCE.

1 qt. fresh cranberries   2 c. boiling water
2 c. sugar   2 orange peels

Place the cranberries, orange peels and boiling water in a large pot. Bring the cranberries and water to a boil. Continue to boil until the skins of the berries have broken. At that point, add the sugar and reduce the heat to simmer the mixture for about 5 to 10 minutes. Chill before serving.

CORNED BEEF AND CABBAGE.

4 lb. corned beef   1 turnip, cubed
4 c. water   2 large onions, chopped
6 potatoes, cut up   1 sm. head cabbage,
6 carrots, peeled and cut up   cut into wedges
1 bay leaf   1/2 tsp. freshly ground pepper

Put the beef in a large dutch oven; add the water and bring to a boil. Cover and simmer over low heat for about 2 hours. Add the potatoes, carrots, turnips, onions and bay leaf. Cook for 30 minutes. Add the cabbage and pepper; cook for another 30 minutes. The meat and vegetables will be tender when done. Serves 4-6.

QUEEN FRITTERS, VANILLA FLAVOR.

1/4 C. butter or margarine	1/2 C. flour
1/2 C. water , boiling	2 eggs
Shortening for frying	1 tsp. vanilla
Powdered sugar for dusting	Jelly or Jam

Place the butter and water in a small saucepan. Once the water begins to boil again, add the flour. Continue stirring, over high heat, until the flour mixture begins to pull away from the saucepan sides. Remove from heat. Add the eggs, one at a time, beating thoroughly after each addition.

In a large Dutch oven, melt enough shortening to deep fry the fritters. Drop the batter by spoonfuls and cook until golden brown and puffy. Place fritters on a paper towel to drain. Remove a small section of the top of the fritter and fill with your favorite jam or jelly. Dust with powdered sugar.

CHARLOTTE DES REUS.

1 pt. cream, whipped	2 egg whites, whipped
2 T. gelatin, dissolved	1 c. sugar
in 1/3 c. hot milk	1 tsp. vanilla & almond extracts
sponge cake*	fruit jelly (warmed)

Gently fold whipped cream, egg whites and sugar together. Refrigerate for 1 hour. Add gelatin, milk and extracts; combine by folding, do not over stir or you will deflate the mixture. Line a mold pan with slices of sponge cake and fill with the cream mixture. Refrigerate for 4 hours. Turn out onto a serving platter. Place a tablespoon of your favorite jelly on a serving plate; spread to the edges of the plate. Cut a slice of the charlotte and put it on the plate. Dust with powdered sugar and garnish with a mint leaf.

* *See recipe on page 216.*

FRUIT CAKE.
(My Great Great Grandmother Osgood's)

Fruit cake is not a dessert that most people think fondly of, including me. However, this recipe is really quite delicious. The good thing about this recipe is that you can substitute any of dried fruits that you like. If raisins, currants, and citron aren't your favorite, try using dried cranberries, peaches, or dates. Experiment! Also, this recipe says to soak the cake in Irish Whiskey, but bourbon, wine, or fruit juice will work well, too.

2 c. sugar	6 tsp. cinnamon
1 c. butter or margarine	2 tsp. cloves
1 c. molasses	3 1/2 c. flour
1 c. golden raisins	1 tsp. baking soda
1 c. raisins	1/2 tsp. salt
1 c. currants	1 c. milk
1 c. citron	2 eggs
1 whole nutmeg, grated	Irish whiskey for soaking

Melt the butter in a large saucepan; add the sugar, molasses, raisins, currants, citron and spices and boil for 6 minutes. Remove from heat and allow to cool.

In a small bowl, sift the flour, soda, and salt together; add the milk and egg and stir to combine. Set aside. Add the cooked sugar and spice mixture to the flour, stir to blend. If the mixture seems too wet, add a little more flour.

Place in a greased tube pan or loaf pan, and bake at 300° for 2 hours. Test for doneness by inserting a toothpick into the cake. If it comes out clean, the cake is done. Allow cake to cool completely before removing it from the pan. The fruit cake must now be mellowed for one to four weeks. To do this, soak a piece of cheesecloth with Irish whiskey and wrap the cake in it. Next, wrap this in foil or plastic wrap. Store the cake in the refrigerator until ready to use. If the cake seems dry, add additional liquor and allow to sit a couple more days.

MINCE PIE.

2 1/2 c. mincemeat   1 double pie crust*, unbaked

MINCEMEAT

1 1/2 lbs. lean beef, cubed   1 c. beef stock
1/4 lb. lard or shortening   1 lb. brown sugar
3 lbs. tart apples, peeled   1 c. cider vinegar
   & cored   1 c. molasses
2 1/2 lbs. raisins   1 1/2 tsp. ground cloves
1/4 c. candied lemon peel   1/2 tsp. allspice
1 T. freshly grated nutmeg   1 1/2 tsp. salt
1 T. cinnamon

Put meat in a large pot, cover with water and simmer until tender. Push the meat, lard or shortening and apples through a food chopper. Place the chopped meat back in the pot, add remaining ingredients and simmer for one hour; stirring often. The mixture can be canned or used immediately. Make about 4 quarts.

Line a 9" pie pan with one pie crust, fill with the mincemeat mixture and place the second pie crust on top to cover. Pinch the dough together and flute the edges. Bake at 400° for 35-40 minutes, or until golden brown. Serve hot.

See recipe on page 146.

SPONGE CAKE.

2 c. sifted flour
1/2 tsp. salt
10 egg yolks
2 T. lemon juice

2 tsp. grated lemon rind
10 egg whites
1 1/4 c. sugar

Sift the flour and salt in a large bowl, three times. Beat the egg yolks until thick and yellow. Add the lemon juice and rind; blend well. In a separate bowl, beat the egg whites until soft peaks form; while whipping, gradually add the sugar. Continue beating until stiff peaks form. Gently fold in the egg yolks, then the flour, 1/4 cup at a time. Be sure not to over beat this mixture, or the cake will not rise properly.

Pour batter into an ungreased 10" tube pan and bake at 350° for 1 hour. Invert the cake pan on a plate, and allow to cool for 1 hour before removing the pan from the cake.

Be sure to cut the cake with a serrated knife so that you do not flatten it. Serve with fresh berries and whipped cream, or cut into three layers and fill with jelly or cream.

FLOATING ISLAND.

4 c. milk
3 T. sugar
6 egg whites, stiffly beaten
   with 2 T. sugar

6 egg yolks, beaten
1 T. vanilla

Place the milk in a double boiler or in a metal bowl over simmering water; heat through. Add the egg whites, do not stir. Leave on water for 2-3 minutes. Gently scoop the egg whites off the milk with a slotted spoon and place on a platter.

In a separate bowl, beat the eggs yolks and sugar to combine. Slowly pour the milk over the eggs and sugar; add the vanilla. Stir to combine. Turn the custard back into the double boiler and cook over medium heat until thick. Turn the custard into a serving dish. Place the egg whites on top of the custard to resemble an island. Chill thoroughly. Serve with a bit of jelly on each plate. Serves 4-6.

BAKED MACARONI & CHEESE.

I always thought that home-made baked macaroni and cheese was hard to make, but it's really not. This recipe is simple and very delicious.

4 c. macaroni, cooked	1/2 tsp. salt
1 c. grated cheddar cheese	pepper to taste
1/3 c. butter, cut into bits	1/2 c. milk or cream

In a buttered baking dish, layer the macaroni, cheese and butter. Sprinkle with salt and pepper. Bake at 350° for 30 minutes, covered. Remove from the oven and pour the milk or cream over. Allow to sit for 10 minutes, stir and serve.

BIBLIOGRAPHY

1. Silver Lady Antiques, Tombstone, AZ. Various rare collectibles and photographs.
2. University of Arizona, Tucson, AZ. 1881-1882 Tombstone City Council record books, St. Paul's Church records, Tombstone Chapter of the Knights of Phythias records, microfilm of *Tombstone Epitaph* July-December 1880, March 1881-July 1882, and the *Daily Record Epitaph* August-November 1885.
3. Arizona Department of Library & Archives, Phoenix, AZ. 1881 Map of Tombstone, 1881 & 1885 Butcher & Live Stock laws, various Pima County leases, and microfilm of *Weekly Nugget* 1879; *Daily Nugget* June-December 1881; *Tombstone Weekly Epitaph* December 1881-December 1882, January 1883; January-August 1890; *Daily Record Epitaph* August-November 1885; *Tombstone Prospector* 3-8-87, 1-11-88, 12-29-88; Arizona Daily Star 1879-1884-various issues. Cochise County Great Registers for 1882 and 1884. Pima County Brand Book-1880.
4. Cochise County, AZ library. Tombstone Epitaph, June 1881.
5. Cochise County, AZ recorder's office. Pima & Cochise County Grantor/Grantee record books, Lessee/Lessor books, Great Registers, 1881 Tombstone map, Bond Book, and Deeds of Real Estate Book.
6. Arizona Pioneer & Historical Society, Tucson, AZ. Medigovich collection, Tombstone letterhead collection, *McKenney's Business Directory 1882-1883*, *Tombstone General & Business 1883-1884 Directory*, and *R.L. Polk's Arizona Gazetteer & Business Directory 1884*.

7. Tombstone Historical Court House photo collection, 1887 tax roll assessment book, and 1887/1888 invoice collection.
8. University of California, Berkeley, Bancroft Library. *Disturnell's 1881 Arizona Gazetteer* and *Tombstone Weekly Nugget*-June 1880.
9. Private collection, *McKenney's Pacific Coast Directory for 1880/1881, Colorado State Gazetteer-1884/1885* and *Southern Pacific Coast Directory-1888/1889.* Copies of drawings from *Arizona Quarterly Illustrated.*
10. Montebello Public Library, Montebello, CA *The LA Evening Express*-June 24, 1881.
11. Geisenhofer recipes, photos, and family history information were provided by Bertha Geisenhofer Dalziel.
12. Library of Congress, Washington, D.C. *Duns Mercantile Directory 1885.*

BUSINESS INDEX

Recipe Index

ORDER FORM

☐ Yes! Please send me the titles I've selected below.

Name_____

Address_____

City_____ State_____ Zip_____

Phone_____Fax_____

Title	Qty.	Each	Total
Taste of Tombstone, A Hearty Helping of History, Sherry Monahan	_____	$16.95	_____
Destination Tombstone, Adventures of a Prospector, Edward Schieffelin, Founder	_____	$14.95	_____
Tombstone, A 60 Minute Audio Magazine (audio cassette) narrated by Timothy R. Walters, True tales of the "town too tough to die."	_____	$12.00	_____
	Subtotal		_____
Arizona residents include 7% sales tax.	Tax		_____
	S&H		$3.00
	TOTAL		_____

Please add $3.00 per order shipping & handling. Foreign orders must be accompanied by a postal money order in U.S. funds.

Look for *Taste of Tombstone* at your favorite bookstore
or send check or money order to:
Royal Spectrum Publishing
P.O. Box 228, Ravia, OK 73455
To order by phone call (405) 371-2904
or fax (405) 371-9792.
Contact Royal Spectrum Publishing about quantity discounts.